HOPSCOTCH
AND
QUEENIE-I-O
A 1960s
Irish Childhood

DAMIAN CORLESS is a journalist, broadcaster and a former editor of *Magill* and *In Dublin*. He has written comedy sketches for BBC TV's classic *Big Train* and RTÉ's award-winning *Stew*. His first play, *Death Wish '16: The GPO* was published in 2016. His acclaimed books include *Looks Like Rain: 9,000 Years of Irish Weather* (2013) and *From Clery's Clock to Wanderly Wagon* (2014), a lively romp through the Irish history you weren't taught at school.

Keep up to date with Damian on Twitter: @DamianCorless

For Sophie, Ollie, Max and Caitlin

HOPSCOTCH
AND
QUEENIE-I-O
A 1960s
Irish Childhood

Damian Corless

The Collins Press

FIRST PUBLISHED IN 2016 BY
The Collins Press
West Link Park
Doughcloyne
Wilton
Cork
T12 N5EF
Ireland

Images courtesy of: 123freevectors.com, Burns Design, facegfx.com,
freepik.com, pixabay.com, retrovectors.com, thegraphicsfairy.com,
vecteezy.com, vintagevectors.com

A CIP record for this book is available from the British Library.

Hardback ISBN: 978-1-84889-292-7
PDF eBook ISBN: 978-1-84889-596-6
EPUB eBook ISBN: 978-1-84889-597-3
Kindle ISBN: 978-1-84889-598-0

Design and typesetting by Burns Design
Typeset in Adobe Garamond
Printed in Lithuania by ScandBook UAB

CONTENTS

CONTENTS

Preface

The children of 1960s Ireland were in-betweeners. Their life experience was sharply different both from that of Irish kids growing up in the grim, stagnant post-war 1950s, and those who would feel the tingly sunburst of colour that came with the more liberated 1970s. In the 1960s the forces of change, ice-bound through the de Valera decades, began slowly to thaw. Ireland edged towards a tipping point, but the more it braced itself for a leap of faith into the modern world, the fiercer the rearguard action from those entrenched elements determined to enforce the old certainties.

The nation's children blinked in this twilight zone between two sundering worlds, but there was only ever going to be one way out, and that way was to rush towards the light of the cathode ray. The arrival of television at the start of the decade was an eye-opener and a game changer, not that earlier generations had been entirely cut off from the outside world.

In the absence of home-grown comics and children's books, generations of Irish kids mired in the grey austerity of Ireland's self-exile had turned for respite to those pillars of British imperialism: Enid Blyton, Billy Bunter, *The Beano, The Dandy* and *The Victor*. From America came Flash Gordon, Buck Rogers and the Wild West cliffhangers (known to many Irish cinema-goers as 'followy-uppers') that were staples of Saturday cinema matinees for decades. But television was something entirely different. As it rapidly replaced the fireplace as the true hearth of the family home, it magnified a thousandfold the wider world beyond Ireland – and the fun and excitement and possibilities that lay out there.

The 1960s brought a reversal of the failed ourselves-alone economics of the previous four decades, and Ireland's kids benefited from the modest lift in their parents' disposable income. Irish youngsters of the 1960s were dished up a wider variety of meals than ever before (in the context of a very narrow national palate), they had more and better toys, while the Sunday drive and the family holiday suddenly became rituals that had never been there for earlier generations.

But it wasn't all convenience foods, caravan parks and salty periwinkles on a pin. School for very many children remained not just drudgery, but a fearsome ordeal. Dickensian teaching methods, discipline and surroundings were the norm. The twin prime functions of primary education as set out by the State were:

1. The school exists to assist and supplement the work of parents in the rearing of their children. Their first duty is to train their children in the fear and love of God. That duty becomes the first purpose of the Primary school.

2. To support the revival of the native tongue through 'the use of the language and awaken a sympathetic disposition to it'.

Before a long-overdue rethink towards the end of the decade, the standard method of teaching Irish was to inflict it on pupils, most of whom never heard a word of it uttered in the real world. There was a widespread belief amongst the teaching profession that the use of physical force was justified in pursuit of this noble cause.

Ireland was a suffocatingly patriarchal society, and girls from early childhood were conditioned to see out their adult years as dutiful wives and mothers. In 1966, a group of Catholic bishops quietly petitioned Taoiseach Seán Lemass to prohibit any girl under the age of eighteen from leaving the country, in order to protect her purity. The government respectfully turned down the proposal on the grounds that it was unenforceable in law, but the fact that the clerics felt it was reasonable to table it in the first place spoke volumes.

Trying to balance two wildly different sets of expectations in this tug-of-war decade was a challenge, but, unburdened by baggage of their own, the kids were all right. Mostly.

All changed, changed utterly – Ireland gets TV

Rationing the new medium to impressionable young minds

Without any doubt, the arrival of television was the single greatest new X factor to impact on Irish life in the 1960s, opening a generation gap between the childhood experience of that decade and all that had gone before. Throughout the 1950s deeply conservative elements embedded in government, the civil service and the rest of Official Ireland had fiercely resisted the coming medium. There were fears that television would act as a Trojan Horse for the cultural recolonisation of a people who had only just reclaimed their heritage after a struggle of centuries.

The trouble for these naysayers was that those living along the border and the eastern seaboard were already gratefully lapping up 'overspill' signals from the BBC and UTV in Northern Ireland, and ITV's Welsh service, Harlech. In the end, reluctantly, Ireland's cultural guardians decided that since they couldn't beat 'em, they'd have to join 'em. If the Irish people were going to be brainwashed by the nefarious goggle-box, the brainwashing should come from our own side.

11

When Telefís Éireann got up and running on the last evening of 1961, the first instincts of those in charge were to ration its bounty, especially to impressionable young minds. With the exception of Sundays, daytime broadcasting would be kept to an absolute minimum throughout the decade, with the sole exception of the schools tutorials provided by Telefís Scoile. The dearth of daytime broadcasting had as much to do with mindset as money.

For thankful Irish mothers, the BBC provided a couple of welcome daytime interludes when an infant could be propped up in a pram, or plopped down on a blanket and lullabied towards the Land of Nod by the magic of *Watch With Mother*. By the start of the decade the show had established its classic weekly lunchtime repertoire of *Picture Book* (Monday), *Andy Pandy* (Tuesday), *Bill & Ben The Flower Pot Men* (Wednesday), *Rag, Tag & Bobtail* (Thursday) and *The Woodentops* (Friday).

With television sets still thin on the ground, the most popular network on the island of Ireland for much of the 1960s was Ulster Television which opened on Halloween night 1959. The station's signature opening chimes played a music-box version of 'The Mountains of Mourne' and were accompanied on screen by oscilloscope lines joining a pattern of dots representing the North's major towns and cities. This symbolism – intended to depict Northern Ireland as a vibrant, confident and, most importantly, separate land – was entirely lost on young southern viewers delighted that *Romper Room* was on the way. Opening the schedules at 4.30 each afternoon, it was presented by Miss Adrienne playing the warm and indulgent schoolteacher to a gaggle of giddy toddlers.

Franchised from the 1950s original, which had taken the United States by storm, *Romper Room* was the happy-clappy kindergarten that every little kid wished was theirs. Early on in each instalment the children would be urged to ask for 'Mister Music, Please'. This was the cue for the in-house ivory tinkler to kick off a jamboree of fun and games. An oversized bumblebee called Mr Do-Bee would provide some gentle instruction in good manners, the kids would run in circles pretending to drive cardboard boxes painted up as fire engines and taxis, and the party wound down when Miss Adrienne produced her Magic Mirror and greeted a handful of lucky viewers in person: 'I can see Mary, and I can see Ivan, and I can see Anne Marie ...'

Young viewers of Telefís Éireann's early evening output got their home-grown entertainment wrapped in the green flag of the Irish language. A noisy, roughly sketched and very static duck called Dáithí Lacha became a staple from 1963, to be quickly followed by *Murphy agus a Chairde,* starring a good-natured Irish-speaking puppet giant. A Gaeilgeoir ventriloquist's dummy called Beartlaí popped up wherever a kids' show needed an extra smattering of Irish. He also co-hosted a series of his own entitled *Seoirse agus Beartlaí* which showcased young local talent.

One of the biggest problems facing the Irish language as the decade progressed was that, more and more, it seemed hopelessly dry and fuddy-duddy for a new TV generation exposed to pop groups, the fashions of Swinging London and the impossibly cool spy adventures of the derring-doers from *The*

Avengers and *The Man From UNCLE*. In an effort to add zest to the native tongue, Telefís Éireann introduced viewers to a trio of glamorous young women who could rattle off the names of all five Rolling Stones on demand, and could slip just as comfortably into skipping through the *tuiseal ginideach* for beginners.

 Two, Máire O'Neill and Aileen Geoghegan, were the presenters of *Buntús Cainte*, a TV tie-in to a state project aimed at giving the ancient tongue a thoroughly modern makeover. Out went solemn histories of saints and scholars meant to improve the recipient, and in came simple phrases which Official Ireland hoped the plain people would sprinkle into their everyday banter. The cartoons that appeared on the show were replicated in a series of booklets, which added a little extra weight to every primary kid's schoolbag in the latter part of the decade.

Despite their best intentions and their best mod gear, the presenters of *Buntús Cainte* always had to battle the fact that, at the back of their young viewer's mind, they and their lessons bore the toxic taint of being associated with school. Not so Bláithín O'Ciobhain who wrote and presented one of the shows most beloved of Irish youngsters and their parents, *Let's Draw With Bláithín*. Through the course of each show Bláithín would drift effortlessly in and out of the native tongue as she encouraged her viewers to set their creative sights a good deal higher than dipping half a potato in paint and stamping it with merry gusto over a sheet of paper.

But even the charisma of three trendy women young enough to be your older sister (in an age when families of ten were common) couldn't shift Paddy Crosbie from his throne as the King of Children's TV. The avuncular Crosbie had created *School Around The Corner* for Radio Éireann in 1954 and it transferred seamlessly to the new television service, as the host coaxed cute performances of song, dance, poetry and prose from clusters of primary school kids. The presenter also composed the theme song of the same name which became part of every child's repertoire. (Reassuringly: 'It hasn't changed at all ... The school around the corner's just the same.') Looking back on a wildly successful first decade in 1965, Crosbie noted with pride: 'The very first boy who appeared on the very first programme in 1954 will be ordained (a priest) this year.'

A great deal of heated debate surrounded the role which the Irish language should play in Telefís Éireann's only sop to daytime weekday viewing, *Telefís Scoile*. The schools service was launched in the spring of 1964 with  physics and chemistry at its heart. These two subjects were chosen precisely because they were deemed very tricky. In other words, there was an acute shortage of competent science teachers in the land, so these subjects were felt most likely to benefit from a proven expert and state-of-the-art graphics. Yet, despite the consensus that physics and chemistry were very hard to grasp, there was still a vocal lobby to add an extra layer of difficulty by having them taught through the medium of Irish. The broadcasters ruled that since the vast majority of schools teaching science were doing so through English, the programmes should be in English.

From mid-decade, Telefís Éireann would go on air at 2 p.m. several times a week for a schools programme, and then close down again until 5.30 p.m. During the summer school holidays, when children were expected to play outside or help on the farm, Telefís Éireann did away entirely with daytime programming, apart from the occasional domestic horse race meeting. For those in single-channel land, the day's viewing began at 6 p.m. with the evening Angelus.

With TV sets few and far between, viewing was often communal, with neighbours dropping in by appointment to watch popular weekly soaps such as *Tolka Row* and *The Riordans*, or special events like the GAA All-Ireland finals or the  Eurovision Song Contest. There were no videocassette recorders, so if you missed a favourite programme you really had missed it. Repeats in the 1960s were almost unknown. Just as pop groups thought it was bad form to include a recent hit single on a new album, broadcasters and viewers here and in Britain felt that repeating a programme was to short-change the audience.

The same degree of customer care did not extend to repackaging cinema films for the small screen, and Telefís Éireann's prime slots were regularly filled with cobwebbed antiques. Mainstream cinema of the day was starting to reflect the so-called Permissive Society, but the moth-eaten films had no truck with that notion. The main reason for padding the schedules with fossilised footage was that it was cheap.

The extreme old age of the films screened by Telefís Éireann was a recurring concern of letter writers to the *RTÉ Guide*. In 1965 one correspondent, signing themselves New Wave, carped: 'Honestly, Telefís Éireann, when are you going to end this nostalgic pathetic little game of yours, showing us the films grandfather brought grandmother to while they were courting? … Still, I suppose it allows of a little game played in our house called Spot The Small-Type Future Stars. It's amazing how many top-liners of the past decade appear as little more than extras on the Telefís Éireann screen.' Another reader picked up the theme the following week, writing: 'Thanks to Telefís Éireann for giving us old-timers an opportunity of seeing our favourite film stars again.'

The letters pages of the *RTÉ Guide*, along with those of the national newspapers, provided a platform for a campaign to augment the six o'clock evening Angelus with a more substantial nightly TV slot devoted to the family rosary. The people behind the campaign favoured clearing the schedules of froth for fifteen minutes around 7 p.m.

In support of the proposal, Mrs Mary Humphries of Cork wrote: '[It is] one of the best suggestions I have ever heard. Those of us with children find it difficult to get any prayers said as there is always something they want to see on the television. But that fifteen minutes for the Rosary would come to them as naturally as any other programme.'

Corresponding from Kildare, Mrs Joseph Kindregan concurred, reflecting: 'We all know that during Cromwell's time it was the Family Rosary that kept the Faith in our land. Surely it would be a great tribute to our forefathers if RTÉ sacrificed just ten minutes to the Rosary. I am the mother of seven young children and I find it difficult to deprive any of them of their special programmes to get them together to say the Rosary. What a blessing and what an advantage for parents it would be if RTÉ showed the Rosary.'

The mandarins of Montrose decided it was not to be. It is worth noting that this was an era when letters to the newspapers and magazines came with a health warning. For every genuine 'Concerned Mother of Ten', there was another even more concerned hoax 'Mother of Ten' whose undercover mission was to ridicule and sabotage the conservative campaign *du jour* by arguing the case to absurd lengths.

One of the finest examples of these hoaxes landed in the office of the Taoiseach. One Francis McConville sent the Taoiseach a radical proposal to achieve 'the complete ignorance of English'. He wrote: 'Only by ensuring that a fresh generation cannot speak English will it be possible to eliminate it as the dominant language.' He explained: 'The solution involves the conversion of the existing primary day schools into primary boarding schools, staffed with Irish-speaking teachers who will impart instruction exclusively through the medium of Irish, and with Irish-speaking domestics who will look after the material well-being of the pupils outside school hours and will provide for their wants as those wants would be otherwise provided for in their own home.' The state's existing schools would be expanded into internment camps for the nation's children. Compulsory purchase orders would be slapped on surrounding buildings, which would be commandeered for dormitories.

The valve-operated television sets of the era were delicate things. After switching on the TV, the viewer would have to wait as long as a minute for the valves to warm up and the screen to flicker into some indication of life. Every TV watcher dreaded hearing a soft *pop* during this warming-up process, when any gathering brightness would drain from the screen, meaning that something had blown. At this point, any father fancying himself as a handyman would remove the back of the heavy casing, risking further damage to the contents. Sometimes the misfiring valve could be replaced, or rejigged, and normal service could resume, but in many cases the night's entertainment was at an end before it had begun and the TV set would have to be lugged back to the rental store as soon as possible.

Because the primitive sets of the day were so fragile, so fickle and so expensive to buy outright, many Irish families had no option but to rent, while many others bought on hire purchase, or HP. The weekly payments to the hire-purchase companies invariably amounted in the long run to far more than the straight cash price of a television set, but the upside was that if your HP TV broke down the hire company would provide a replacement set while yours was in the repair shop.

The government's Household Budget Inquiry for 1965–66 attempted to take a snapshot of how urban Irish households were spending their money. In one category covering discretionary spending, the rent of a television and/or wireless set came in at Number Three on the list. This was just ahead of the amount disbursed in pocket money, but a long way behind 'church and charity contributions' in first place, and 'betting payments, less winnings, pools etc.' in second.

In addition to buying outright, buying via hire purchase or renting, there was for a while a fourth option. Advertisements for a long-forgotten pay-per-view system appeared in the Irish newspapers shortly after Telefís Éireann went on air. Featuring a drawing of a smiling family group, one proclaimed 'They're Happy They've Got TV Slot '. The sales pitch continued: 'You pay as you view – and there's a rebate too! Two shillings in the slot covers everything.' The copywriter elaborated:

> Thousands of viewers are finding that Slot TV helps them save for the things they've always wanted while watching television.
>
> ALL THE FAMILY SHARE THE COST
>
> If the menfolk want to watch boxing or football, they pay. If the mother's fancy turns to Women's Hour, she pays. And if the youngsters want to watch Westerns – well, it's up to them.
>
> THERE'S A REBATE TOO!
>
> Everything in the meter above a low minimum charge is refunded, so you actually save as you view!
>
> THE COIN IN THE SLOT LOOKS AFTER EVERYTHING
>
> Your new, latest-ever 19-inch television set is installed and maintained free of cost – and we guarantee a 'never without a set' service.

Slot TV had agents in Dublin, Laois and Mayo, but the idea that Daddy, Mammy and the kids would pay for their shows in individual portions ran against the grain, and TV watching remained a negotiated family affair.

Be kind to animals and never point a loaded gun at anyone

Some rules of behaviour for the Sixties Child

The trappings of an egalitarian Republic could not disguise the fact that the class system was alive and well in a stratified society where conformity was king and the so-called safety valve of mass emigration showed an open door to malcontents. The message drummed into children by Church and state, most often with the say-so of parents, was to knuckle down and fit in. In this respect, the defining word of the decade was Deference.

The Christian Brothers set out the ground rules in their 1962 pamphlet *Courtesy For Boys and Girls*. The following excerpts illustrate the fact that, at least through the early years of the decade, small children were expected to act like miniature adúlts.

AT HOME

Mother has been taking care of us since we were babies. Our troubles, worries and pains will always be hers too. And don't forget your father. He works hard from Monday to Saturday and from year to year in order to provide for you the clothes, food, pocket money etc. that you are so happy to have. His earnings pay the rent, light the fires, fill the pots and pans, repair boots and shoes, keep the radio playing and give you treats now and then.

When visitors are received in your home, help to put away the hats and coats and return them when the visitors depart. Place a chair for the visitor and be ready to open the door for him when leaving. If the visitor is alone you should offer to see him to the bus or train, or all the way home if the distance is short.

Sitting: leave the more comfortable chairs for your elders and for visitors. It is rude to sit so close to the fire that the heat is cut off from others.

At Table

Say Grace before and after meals. As a general rule, speak only to those who sit next to you or opposite you.

Cleanliness & Dress

Your body is the Temple of the Holy Ghost and, please God, will one day enjoy the happiness of Heaven. Consequently you should make every effort to keep your body clean and properly attired.

Take a bath regularly.

Use a nailbrush or file every morning. Leave no black rims!

Have your hair cut and arranged in a style suited to your age. As far as possible, attend to your hair in private only.

DEPORTMENT

Practise an easy, graceful way of standing – head erect, back straight but not stiff, feet slightly apart and hands lightly held in front or at back, or hanging naturally by the sides.

When walking, keep your head up and your shoulders back, swing your arms lightly close to your sides. Do not drag your feet or take too long a step.

Take care not to develop peculiar mannerisms such as continual fiddling with, or twirling, your fingers.

Boys! Show great respect and reverence for women and girls.

Girls! Prove yourself worthy of that respect by your conduct, deportment and dress.

CONVERSATION

Vulgar words or slang expressions are never heard from the lips of a courteous boy or girl.

If you tell a joke, be careful that it is clean and, of course, funny.

On the telephone: it is very bad manners to listen to private conversations, to stand near a person using the telephone, to

turn on the radio or television when people are having a chat or to interrupt another's talk. When using the telephone ... cut down the conversation – and the telephone bill! Normally it is the privilege of the person who makes the call to terminate it.

God's House – The Church

Take your place as near the Sanctuary as possible. Girls should have their heads covered and they should take care that their headscarves are not such as to be a distraction to others. Avoid coughing except when necessary. It is very rude to read a prayerbook during the sermon.

At School

You should attend to your lessons at school, use your time there well, and so help the teacher whose task is to train you to be a good Catholic and an honourable and responsible citizen.

If you are near the door when a teacher or visitor is about to enter or leave, open the door and hold it open until he (or she) shall have passed through.

Stand when a visitor enters the classroom and remain standing until told to be seated.

It is very unkind and very rude to refuse to speak to a companion just because you have had a quarrel. It is sad to hear a girl say: 'I'm not speaking to her' – and some boys play this silly game too.

In Public

When walking on a footpath keep to the right. Boys, however, should give ladies the inside position.

Some points here for boys wearing caps. They should raise their caps as a sign of respect:

(a) When they pass a Church or cemetery

(b) When they meet a Priest, Brother or Nun, or a lady whom they know

(c) When they are walking with a lady (mother, sister, friend etc.) and someone salutes her

(d) When they meet a friend with a lady – for example a classmate walking with his mother

(e) When they are spoken to by a lady or by any person of high rank. They should also raise their caps when they finish speaking to such people

(f) When they have done a lady some little service, for example, handing her a glove which she has dropped. (The cap is raised by the hand further away from the person saluted.)

(g) When the National Anthem of their own, or of any other country is being played or sung in public. They should then stand erect, holding their caps in the right hand over the heart. This is also done by bystanders when the National Flag is carried in procession.

Visits to Friends

Unless you are invited to sit in an armchair, chose an ordinary chair. Do not sit until you are asked.

If, while seated, you are addressed by a lady or a person of rank who is standing, stand up to reply.

If you are introduced to an Archbishop or Bishop you should go down on one knee, take his hand lightly and kiss his ring. An Archbishop is addressed as 'Your Grace' and a Bishop as 'My Lord'.

BEFORE WE GO

Be kind to animals. Do not overload, beat or torment them.

Girls should be careful not to stand too near a fire – the draught may cause their dresses to catch fire.

Boys need to be careful in handling knives, pellet guns etc. Never point a loaded gun at anyone. Better still, leave these things aside altogether; they are dangerous as playthings.

For girls only

Intermediate Certificate Domestic Science questions

Q: Write detailed instructions for the care and cleaning of each of the following:

(a) Kitchen sink

(b) Waste bin

(c) Kitchen cutlery

(d) Glassware

(e) Outdoor shoes

List the kitchen cloths necessary for a household of six persons.

Q: Write notes on the use, care and cleaning of the sewing machine. State the causes of the following faults in machining, and mention how each would be rectified.

(a) Material puckering

(b) Stitches looping

(c) Thread breaking

Q: Compile a suitable menu for a three-course dinner in Winter. Give quantities of the ingredients required for the main course for a family of four adults. State the approximate cost of each course on the menu. Give the recipe together with method of making the meat course or a substitute dish selected for the main course.

Q: What points should guide you in your choice of a new outfit for outdoor wear? Give general rules for the care and storage of your personal clothing. Discuss the advantages and disadvantages of possessing a small versus a large quantity of clothes for outdoor wear.

Q: Plan, and set out in menu form, a nourishing breakfast suitable for schoolchildren on a cold morning in Winter. State the quantities of ingredients which would be required for the meal suggested for four children.

Assuming the breakfast is to be served for 8.30 a.m., give a time plan of the order of work which should be followed when preparing the meal. Give instructions for cleaning the breakfast table and for washing up and putting away the breakfast ware and cooking utensils used.

Q: Describe in detail with the aid of clear diagrams how any two of the following should be worked.

(a) Finishing the neck edge of an undergarment by the use of bias binding.

(b) Working a buttonhole on a cotton frock.

(c) Attaching lace to the hemline of a slip by means of fancy stitching.

Intermediate Certificate Domestic Science papers 1960, 1964 and 1968. Up to a curriculum change in 1967 the heading of the exam paper included, in brackets, For Girls Only.

A–Z

A

Aspro Ireland's top selling pain-relief tablet.
According to the adverts: 'Medical science has now

proved that the Aspro formula is
the world's most effective pain
reliever.' Although it was the
world's best-selling pain-relief
medicine throughout the 1960s,
it was not until 1971 that English
pharmacologist John Vane
discovered how aspirin actually
works, for which he won a
Nobel prize.

Avon Lady She called to the door trying to sell
your mother cosmetics and/or recruit your mother to
open her home to friends and neighbours for the
purpose of hawking Avon products.

Aztec Bar Made of chocolate, nougatine and
caramel, the Aztec first appeared in 1967 but lasted
just eleven years. For the launch, life-sized Aztec
warriors made of cardboard
stood guard outside
shops.

B

Balsa Wood The basis of countless different flatpack model aircraft free with the English comics, but usually not to Irish readers.

'Be the Hokey' Catchphrase of Tom Riordan, rough-hewn soap patriarch of *The Riordans*.

Belvedere Bond 'Ireland's finest stationery'.

Biafra Classroom and church collections were taken up to aid malnourished child victims living in Nigeria's secessionist province before it was crushed and reintegrated in 1970. A special performance of the showbiz revue *Gaels of Laughter '68* at Dublin's Gaiety Theatre channelled all proceeds 'to aid the nuns in Biafra'.

Bill Sikes Played with terrifying conviction by Oliver Reed, the vicious woman-beating Sikes from the screen musical *Oliver!* struck fear and revulsion into small children like no other hate figure of the day.

Brendan O'Reilly Former Irish High Jump champion nicknamed Daddy Longlegs, O'Reilly read out the Saturday evening sports results, and hosted the TV drill class *Sport and You* and the music show *The Life of O'Reilly* (see p. 165)

Chips with everything

Erin Supermash, packet curries & pester power

Whether eating in or dining out, food in Ireland during the early 1960s was a dull and deeply unadventurous affair for adults and children alike. The situation had improved by the close of the decade, but not much. Writing in his 1964 book *Ireland*, American author J. McCarthy portrayed the typical family meal as a joyless experience, 'a necessary chore rather than an artistic ceremony, and the Irishman will usually eat everything put in front of him without bothering overmuch about its flavour or seasoning'. Surveying the country's very limited restaurant scene in March 1963, *Creation* magazine lamented that nine out of ten people visiting a restaurant would order 'steak every time, and seven out of ten men will order chips every time'. A plate of steak and chips with a bottle of either Blue Nun or Black Tower wine was pricey, making it a rare treat for most adults that usually warranted getting dressed up to the nines and chartering a babysitter for the evening.

In mid-decade the government carried out a Household Budget Inquiry spanning 1965 and 1966. The survey was confined to urban Ireland and the compilers later admitted their methods were flawed, but it still provides the best picture we have of where the average annual household income of £4,795 was going.

In a decade when a great many families did not have a car, many Irish households depended on the delivery rounds of the milkman, the breadman and the vegetable man to keep them well stocked with the basics. The inquiry found that the average family spent ten times as much on white bread as on brown, and ten times more on butter than the only spread available, margarine, despite the fact that The Stork Cookery Service, promising 'recipes for all occasions', was patrolling the country sponsoring cooking and baking seminars for housewives. Apart from attempting to promote margarine as superior to butter on the grounds that it was softer and more spreadable, the Stork gatherings centred on the nationwide switch from cooking on the traditional turf-stoked hob to cooking with gas and electricity. The new makes of oven allowed for a wider versatility and ambition in the housewife chef.

The main meal of the day, which was often served at lunchtime, almost always included some manner of meat. Chicken was expensive, and chicken for Sunday lunch was widely regarded by Ireland's kids as a great treat. Towards the end of the decade, as more producers turned to battery farming, chicken started to tumble in price and appear more frequently on the Irish dining table. Fresh fish was cheap and abundant but rarely eaten except in observance of the Catholic Church's Friday fast which forbade meat. Fresh fish was the focus of food snobbery, partly *because* it was so cheap and abundant, and because it was associated with penance. Tinned salmon, on the other hand, was every food snob's delight, to be served up when there were guests to impress. The household survey found that the average Irish family spent more on tinned salmon than any single type of fresh fish bar whiting.

Tinned fruit enjoyed a similar prestige in 1960s Irish households. After apples, oranges and bananas, all the best-selling fruit varieties came in cans, usually soused in sickly sweet syrup. Served with almost every main dish, potatoes were consumed in vast quantities, followed in descending order by cabbage, tomatoes, carrots, onions and dried peas. While the fridge was making an appearance in more homes every year, it was still the exception rather than the rule. Many households relied on a larder cupboard to keep milk, butter and vegetables relatively cool. In homes without a fridge, frozen peas would not keep, while items like ice cream and fish fingers had to be consumed more or less straight from the shop. Launched in 1955, Birds Eye Fish Fingers were a universal children's favourite by the 1960s, accounting for some ten per cent of all the fish purchased in Ireland.

Irish youngsters, like their parents, consumed vast amounts of refined sugar in their tea, and sprinkled on their breakfast cereals and anything else that would take it including, at the most sickly end of the scale, two slices of buttered bread to make the sugar sandwich. In most households coffee was consumed only, if at all, as a rare treat, but the teapots of Ireland gushed forth boundlessly from breakfast to bedtime. Tea came loose

from the packet and was of much higher quality than the teabags that would gradually take over from the 1970s on when the manufacturers would give teabags an almighty push, having twigged from the start that they could get away with filling the little gauze pillows with the fannings and dust leftovers of the good leaves – and charge much the same price. Giving up sugared tea for Lent was a standard act of self-denial for 1960s children and adults alike.

The only fast-food treat available was fish and chips from a chipper or perhaps, on a trip to the seaside, a cluster of boiled periwinkles served in a cone of greaseproof paper. Not to every child's taste, the salty green sea snails were extracted from their shells with the aid of a pin provided by the stall vendor. Most of the chips consumed by Irish children came from the kitchen chip pan which was boiled up on Friday evenings in many households. Mazola corn oil was a brand leader on the back of its long-running TV adverts. The catchphrase 'Frying tonight with Mazola' was famously sent-up by Kenneth Williams – submerging into a vat of boiling oil – in the 1966 comedy classic *Carry On Screaming*. Olive oil, on the other hand, was almost unknown in Ireland of the 1960s. It was generally used only as a treatment for ear infections and only available from chemists in miniature bottles.

Although the first microwave oven had been patented in 1945, these space-age devices would not become part of the kitchen furniture until the 1980s. In the absence of micro-wavable meals, convenience foods of the 1960s tended to be both inconvenient and less appetising than the picture on the box. The popular Vesta Chicken Curry consisted of a bag of rice that needed boiling, and a packet of assorted granules the consistency of gravel. In a decade when milk was delivered in bottles, and milkmen frequently went on strike, many households kept an emergency supply of either condensed milk the consistency of thick cream, or powdered milk which tasted like chalk.

By far the most popular form of convenience food in the 1960s also came in powdered form. Instant mashed potato was a huge favourite with the nation's children, although again the process of adding boiling water, stirring vigorously and then having to wash stubborn gunk from a messy pot meant that the term 'instant' was a misnomer. The country's potato growers were furious that people were spending vast amounts on imported powder.

Fuming in the Dáil chamber, one TD complained: 'In my home town Knorr Instant Potato, Fry-Cadbury's Smash and Erin Supermash are on sale on the one shelf in the one supermarket. I think it is a public disgrace that something was not done to stop the vultures from outside coming to this country and completely annihilating our processed food industry.' He thundered that the two imported brands were priced cheaper than the home-produced Erin mash.

In the capital, one welcome item of less-inconvenient food, provided by the supermarkets that sprang up in the latter part of the decade, was properly digestible meat. A shocking survey by the Agricultural Institute established that Dublin's steak-eaters needed to develop jaws able to exert a force of 34lb, as opposed to the usual 22lb in rural areas. In other words, the city's butchers in the 1960s were dumping leathery meat on customers who, having become accustomed to this abuse over generations, expected no better.

Other Sixties ready-to-go innovations included Heinz tinned ravioli and spaghetti hoops, and, for the ultimate in ready-made sugary luxury, the ice cream in a sponge: the arctic roll.

Like her or loathe her, Irish youngsters had no choice but to endure the TV cookery escapades of Monica Sheridan because Monica's shows like *Home For Tea* were required viewing for every dutiful housewife. Monica was a celebrity chef long before the term was coined. Befitting the unadventurous tastes of the Irish nation, Monica's recipes rarely strayed far from the meat-and-two-veg template, usually accompanied by a dessert that explored the versatility of tinned fruit. But Monica's lack of ambition in the kitchen merely reflected the dinnertime demands of the typical Irish husband and children. Sometimes, perhaps, the severe limitation of those demands got to her. Having sleepwalked through yet another crushingly pedestrian magazine column, she signed off: 'I'm sure you all know how to make the old-fashioned tripe and onions, so I won't burden you with that recipe.'

The 1960s heralded the advent of Pester Power at the Irish
 breakfast table. The trio of elves called Snap, Crackle and Pop had grinned out from the front of Rice Krispies packs since the 1930s, but on the cusp of the 1960s they were given a makeover to render them even more appealing to children. After decades as a trio of elderly big-nosed, big-eared creatures, the elves were reinvented as the young, good-looking, fun-loving stars of catchy TV adverts. The trick worked and Irish kids responded. Other characters who made the leap from the cereal box to the role of small-screen salesman included Tony the Tiger,

the purring spokesfeline for Kellogg's Sugar Frosted Flakes. Kellogg's launched Coco Pops in 1961, initially fronted by Mister Jinks from Hanna-Barbera's popular cartoon *Pixie and Dixie and Mr Jinks*. The role of peddling Coco Pops to Irish and British kids passed later in the decade to Sweep, the mongrel glove puppet from *The Sooty Show* who communicated through a kazoo-like squeak.

For the latter years of the 1960s, the mothers of Ireland would herd their offspring around the television set on one special night of the year for the Calor Housewife of the Year jamboree. Gay Byrne hosted this annual Lovely Girls triathlon for the mature Irishwoman, and at its heart was the finalists' ability to rustle up a tasty meal for their hubby and kids. With the cookery task out of the way, the contestants were given a dab of make-up and wheeled back out to tell how they had trapped their man. Having established their desirability in the kitchen and the ballroom, they closed with a party piece that might be a song, or a jig, or a poem in Irish.

The contest was a big ratings draw for decades, before it was shot down by both sides. On the one side were those traditionalists carping that the competition had been debased because far too many women with jobs outside the home were taking part, shutting out 'real' stay-at-home mothers. Taking potshots from the other side were the feminists and the PC lobby who said that the show was outdated and demeaning to women. The morning after what turned out to be the final show, a caller phoned RTÉ to protest that most of the glammed-up finalists 'would never get down on their knees to scrub the floor'.

Ten favourite children's novelty songs

'Goodness Gracious Me' – Peter Sellers and Sophia Loren
Every kid loved this novelty song where Sellers' doctor caused Loren's heart to go 'boom boody-boom boody-boom boody-boom boody-boom boody-boom boody-boom-boom-boom'.

'Hello Mudduh, Hello Fadduh!' – Alan Sherman
A boy writes home from summer camp where his bunkmate has contracted malaria and the rescuers are out searching for missing children.

'Itsy Bitsy Teenie Weenie Yellow Polka Dot Bikini' – Brian Hyland
Having finally steeled herself to get in for a swim, a bashful young lady in a skimpy swimsuit is then afraid to come out of the water.

'Lily The Pink' – Scaffold
Featuring Elton John, Graham Nash, Tim Rice and Cream's Jack Bruce, this referenced Mr Frears' sticky-out ears and Jennifer Eccles' terrible freckles.

'Little Boxes' – PETE SEEGER
Kids thought this just a nonsense ditty about little boxes 'all made out of ticky tacky and they all look the same', but its serious adult theme was bad housing.

'Three Wheels On My Wagon' – THE NEW CHRISTY MINSTRELS
Burt Bacharach writes his first hit tune as a Wild West pioneer family flee hostile Cherokees with the wheels falling off their wagon.

'Wand'rin' Star' – LEE MARVIN
Hollywood star Lee Marvin croaks his way through this cowboy epic, from the hit film *Paint Your Wagon,* about the pros and cons of campfire life under the open skies. Clint Eastwood's flip-side, 'I Talk to the Trees', also tickled young fancies.

'The Unicorn' – THE IRISH ROVERS
As told by Shel Silverstein and Canada's Irish Rovers, the loveliest animal of all wasn't gifted with brains, and went extinct after missing the sailing of Noah's Ark.

'Yellow Submarine' – THE BEATLES
Ringo takes the lead on this infectious McCartney song where the submarine represents The Beatles' feeling of being trapped by their fame.

'Yummy Yummy Yummy' – OHIO EXPRESS
This saccharine bubblegum song pointed out that love is such a sweet thing it's good enough to eat, and so on and so forth.

Nazi-bashing nuns empty the classrooms

The school excursion to see *The Sound of Music*

How do you solve a problem like Maria? That was a real-life question facing the makers of the 1965 blockbuster *The Sound of Music*. The Maria in question was Maria Von Trapp, one of seven singing siblings to be immortalised on screen. The problem was that the film already had a Maria, played by its big-ticket star Julie Andrews. So, not letting the facts get in the way of a good story, the producers renamed the little Maria as Louisa. And the tinkering didn't stop there. Speaking many years later, Maria Jnr reflected: 'It's a nice story, but it's not really *our* story.'

Indeed, but the biggest family blockbuster of the 1960s is one of the best-known stories in the history of cinema. Girl meets man. Man hires girl as governess for his clatter of kids. Girl falls for man, while liberating the household from its buttoned-down gloom through the magic of song and dance. Girl marries man. They all live happily ever after.

Any number of documentary makers and cultural historians will attest that the Swinging Sixties were a decade when the world embraced free love, mind-expanding pursuits and far-out fashions, but the statistics beg to differ. Love-ins, scraggy hair and weird new music scared the living daylights out of the larger part of society, who ran for the comfort of old certainties and family values.

 *The Sound of Music* had those in spades, and it trounced The Beatles film *Help!* at the box office. To judge by the ten top-grossing films of 1965, it would be easy to dismiss the youth revolution as a hoax. They included two westerns, the Russian potboiler *Doctor Zhivago*, Disney's *That Darn Cat*, and the Biblical epic *The Greatest Story Ever Told*.

True, The Beatles' *Sergeant Pepper* would narrowly pip *The Sound of Music* soundtrack as the decade's best-selling record, most probably because millions of households already had the Broadway cast album. In Catholic Ireland the film's tale of Nazi-bashing nuns emptied a thousand classrooms, as teachers (many of them nuns) arranged school outings so their young charges could witness what for many sisters was the real greatest story ever told.

But, as the real Maria Von Trapp suggested, the film took numerous liberties with the known facts and, when it came out, the real Von Trapp children were dismayed to see their tender and loving father, Georg, portrayed as a stern, aloof disciplinarian. The Julie Andrews character was also distorted beyond recognition. The real-life governess hired by Georg was a strict enforcer, a religious hardliner and quick to anger.

Except that Maria Augusta Kutschera never was hired as a governess in the first place. She was taken on as a nanny to care just for Maria Jnr who was recovering from a serious illness and had to stay home from school.

And the governess didn't fall head over heels for Georg, as the film tells it. In fact, she admitted in her autobiography (on which the musical was based) that she fell in love with the children and wed Georg to be close to them. The couple married in 1927, long before the Nazi annexation of Austria in 1938 which is when the film sets the romance.

By the time the jackboots stomped in, the family had become well-known professional performers, though not by choice. Georg's fortune had been wiped out in the Great Depression, forcing him to put his sons and daughters on the stage. Georg refused to fly the swastika over his home, and family legend says he turned down an invitation to entertain Hitler.

And Maria the problem nun didn't implant the children's love of music. They were highly accomplished before her arrival. And one of the film's most famous scenes – where they escape to Switzerland carrying their instruments – simply didn't happen. In fact they went to Italy, with no drama.

The film's fairy-tale ending had no room for the trauma that confronted them upon arrival in the United States. They were detained at Ellis Island by Immigration. Facing the grim prospect of deportation back to Nazi Austria, they made contact with a businessman who was a fan. He intervened and they eventually made a new start in Vermont, touring constantly.

Georg died in 1947, and the widowed Maria Snr published her life story two years later. It became the basis of the Broadway musical and the film, and brought the Von Trapps great fame and fortune. Questions remain, however, as to how much tinkering the problematic Maria Snr did with the truth long before Hollywood got its mitts on her story. The nunnery at Nonnberg, key to Maria's account, has strongly insisted that its detailed records show no sign of her ever being there.

Other holes in the nun's tale suggest that Maria Snr said more than her prayers, but for countless Irish schoolchildren of the 1960s she will always be fondly remembered as the Julie Andrews' character who got them a half-day off school.

Top family films 1960

A DOG OF FLANDERS
Starring Donald Crisp, David Ladd

Based on a much-loved novel, this children's classic follows the trials and tribulations of Nello (David Ladd) in nineteenth-century Antwerp. Nello is being raised by his grandfather and life is a struggle. They make ends meet, just about, by delivering milk from a cart with the aid of their dog, Patrasche. When his grandfather dies, Nello is taken under the wing of a painter who encourages him to follow his dream to become an artist, and everyone lives happily ever after (in stark contrast to the novel, in which boy and dog freeze to death). David Ladd would grow up to marry Cheryl Stoppelmoor who would find global fame as Cheryl Ladd, star of that TV favourite with 1970s youngsters and their dads, *Charlie's Angels*.

THE MAGNIFICENT SEVEN
Starring Yul Brunner, Steve McQueen, Eli Wallach, James Coburn

Charles Bronson lined up amongst the seven as Bernardo O'Reilly, a gunfighter of Irish-Mexican stock who has seen better days. Led by the veteran gunslinger Chris Adams, played by Yul Brunner, the seven join forces to protect a Mexican village from a gang of cruel bandits. After many heated

arguments, decency and heroism triumph and the hired guns take on the far superior numbers of the bandit gang. While boys of all ages flocked to the film, it was slammed by the critics. One of the seven, Robert Vaughn, would go on to be a superstar of Sixties kids' TV as Napoleon Solo in *The Man From UNCLE*.

POLLYANNA
Starring Hayley Mills, Jane Wyman and Karl Malden

Shining in the lead role, young Hayley Mills won an Academy Juvenile Award for her portrayal of an orphaned twelve-year-old with a gift for accentuating the positive. Walt Disney delivered yet another children's classic, managing to turn a tearjerker into one of the feel-good films of the decade. Despite its evident qualities, the film was a relative flop at the box office. A disappointed Disney reflected: 'I think the picture would have done better with a different title. Girls and women went to it, but men tended to stay away because it sounded sweet and sickly.'

SPARTACUS
Starring Kirk Douglas, Laurence Olivier, Jean Simmons, Tony Curtis

While not strictly a children's film, Stanley Kubrick's Oscar-laden swords 'n' sandals epic won the hearts of millions of boys who were completely unaware of its backstage political subtext. The screenplay, about a little man taking on a great empire, was written under an alias by Dalton Trumbo who was himself fighting back against the might of Hollywood, having being blacklisted for suspected communist sympathies. The decision by Kirk Douglas, who played the leader of the slave revolt, to reveal Trumbo as the writer of the screenplay, was instrumental in bringing down the blacklist system. On its release, cinemas were picketed in the US by anti-communist groups such as the National League of Decency, to little effect.

THE SWISS FAMILY ROBINSON
Starring John Mills, Dorothy McGuire

The celebrated British actor John Mills would spend the close of the 1960s stranded in Kerry as David Lean's Irish epic *Ryan's Daughter* ran onto the rocks, but Mills began the decade in happier circumstances as the swashbuckling father of a family shipwrecked on a tropical island. A huge critical and commercial success, *The Swiss Family Robinson* was lauded on its release by *The New York Times* which said: 'It's hard to imagine how the picture could be better as a rousing, humorous and gentle-hearted tale of family love amid primitive isolation and dangers.'

Minnie skirts have brought storms, earthquakes

Clothing the nation's children

One of the great unsung icons of 1960s Ireland was the sewing machine. The main reason it was unsung is because it was all about women. It remained hidden away from public view in a corner of the kitchen or parlour, of no interest to men, until they wanted something made or mended. The pedal-powered sewing machine had been a feature of Irish home life for generations, but in the 1960s the final stages of the long-running Rural Electrification Scheme dovetailed neatly with the arrival of affordable electrified models designed for home use.

While much children's clothing was store-bought, garments were kept in long service through relentless home maintenance. While the bulk of this repair work fell to the mother, girls were encouraged to chip in from as soon as they could usefully manipulate sewing or knitting needles.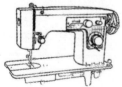

As a young girl in the 1960s west of Ireland, Mary McGlynn remembers her mother as a devoted member of the Irish Countrywomen's Association (ICA), which held evening gatherings all over the country, spreading useful information on everything from how to get the best out of the new electric appliances to making the most out of old clothes. Mary recalls: 'The women back then were all such wonderful home makers and they were so self-sufficient. They did so much with their hands. We talk today about recycling but the women in those days recycled practically everything. They would make patchwork quilts for use in the home using pieces of skirt, or a blouse, or an item of clothing that was worn to the point that you couldn't wear it any more, but ninety per cent of the material was okay to recycle.

'And they did a lot of knitting too. When the kids got too big for their jumpers, their mothers would rip them apart and knit them back together so they might last another few months before you'd have to buy a new one. People have this idea that the members of the ICA just got together to have a natter over tea and buns, but they were very, very self-sufficient.

'Rural electrification would have come to my village on the western seaboard in the early 1960s. That was a huge plus for the women in the home. It meant they could now get a washing machine and an electric cooker. They would have seen all these recipes for various dishes in the magazines and newspapers, but they were dishes that they could never cook on their ancient range. Before the coming of electric light, the house would have been lit by lamps and candles, but electric light was much better for doing their sewing and knitting.'

This thrifty self-sufficiency and mend-and-make-do approach to clothing was by no means confined to rural Ireland. The government's Household Budget Inquiry covering 1965–66 was exclusively confined to urban Ireland, and showed similar tailoring and recycling patterns. The spending survey ranked the top five clothing outgoings as Footwear, Cardigans/Jumpers,

Overcoats, Stockings and Materials For Women's And Girls' Clothing. Listed under Personal Services, a different budgetary top five included Shoe Repairs and Dyeing & Cleaning. The disposable age was a long way off for Ireland in the 1960s, and with it the godsend to Irish mothers that would one day be the disposable nappy. Across the nation washing lines drooped under the dead weight of soggy nappies hung out to dry.

For many Irish Catholic boys, their first experience of wearing long trousers would have been at around the age of twelve when they were fitted out in their Confirmation suit. Up to that, short pants and tightly cropped hair were the general rule. In his day-to-day get-up, the average young Irish boy of the 1960s looked pretty much like he could have been plucked straight from the pages of *The Beano* or *The Dandy*.

For girls, clothes were more complex, but more interesting too. The mid-decade Household Budget Inquiry found that the average spend on store-bought clothes went 1. Women's; 2. Men's; 3. Boys'; 4. Girls'. Less was spent on off-the-peg clothes for girls because their industrious mothers were well able to make dresses for them, and by the age of twelve or so, the girls were expected to possess the skills to have a go at it themselves. With neither access to the latest voguish fashions from Carnaby Street, nor the means to buy them in any case, many Irish girls in their early teens simply manufactured their own fab gear on the kitchen table. It was a task they'd been reared for. A toy sewing machine featured in a great many letters to Santa during the decade. Knitting and sewing were a key part of the school curriculum for girls, and one of the few pop shows on Irish radio was the

Singer Sewing Machine Show every Tuesday on the nation's lone radio station.

One of the fashion crazes to come out of Carnaby Street as the Sixties got into full swing was the crochet dress. Modelled by style icons like Twiggy and Sharon Tate, it looked like the much younger, much prettier sibling of the Aran sweater. And when the mothers of Ireland weren't dressing their little daughters up to the nines in homespun wool creations, their fall-back role model throughout the 1960s was Jacqueline Kennedy, wife of, and then widow of, Irish-American President John F. Kennedy.

The word 'unisex' first entered circulation in the late 1960s, although no one can say with certainty who coined the term. While the word was not heard in Ireland at the time (any word featuring, or consisting entirely of 'sex' was to be avoided in polite conversation), several trendy clothing items were common to both boys and girls. These included duffle coats, casual pigskin Hush Puppies, and berets for the endless school, civic and Church parades that were a feature of every schoolchild's life. The Hush Puppies brand got a credibility boost with the youth in 1965 after  the manufacturers claimed that the crepe rubber soles on their product saved the life of Rolling Stone Keith Richards. The story went that Keef's guitar brushed off an ungrounded microphone and the rocker was knocked unconscious, with attending medics concluding that his shoes had insulated him from the full, potentially lethal, shock.

The clothes fad that caused the biggest sensation, and provoked the greatest condemnation, throughout the entire decade was the

miniskirt which rose, and rose, and rose from the Swinging London scene. For decades, young girls in Ireland had been wearing short dresses until they entered their teens, but when it became fashionable to continue with the fashion at thirteen, fourteen, fifteen and beyond, the mini became a burning cause célèbre for guardians of decency.

In 1967, for instance, a party of VIPs stepping off a flight from the States were quick to register their dismay at Ireland's tolerance of, and enthusiasm for, this latest fad. According to the *Sunday Press*: 'Disgust at the sight of so many miniskirts was expressed by the American contenders for the Rose of Tralee title when they flew into Shannon Airport ... "I don't even own a mini" said Miss New York.'

Two years earlier in 1965 the sudden rise of the miniskirt provoked an American woman to write to Taoiseach Seán Lemass fearing the end of the world was nigh: 'What I want to ask you is if the women and girls in Catholic Ireland are wearing "Minnie dresses" and tight pants and "minnie skirts"? Here in the USA our women in their "minnie dresses" have brought God's displeasure. We have had storms, earthquakes.'

Ireland remained an earthquake-free zone through to the end of the decade, by which time the miniskirt had become risibly unhip and passé. The early years of the 1970s would belong to the mini's polar extreme, the maxi-dress.

A–Z

C

Car Registrations A hobby of almost every small Irish boy of the 1960s was to choose a roadside spot and write down the registration of every vehicle that passed over a given period, along with details of the make and colour. According to the British comics, the pay-off for noting down car reg. numbers was invariably a large cash reward for foiling a bank robbery or leading the police to a villains' lair. With criminal gangs thin on the ground in 1960s Ireland, most small boys moved swiftly on to the next passing fad.

Catechism Every Catholic primary pupil had to learn by rote questions such as Q: 'At what age are children obliged to go to Confession?' A: 'Children are obliged to go to Confession as soon as they are capable of committing sin – that is, when they come to the use of reason, which is generally supposed to be about the age of seven years.'

'Ceement Pond' The name given by the magnificently thick Jethro Bodine to the swimming pool in his nouveau riche bumpkin family's newly acquired Hollywood mansion. *The Beverly Hillbillies* was an abiding children's favourite from its first Irish airing in 1963.

Child Catcher Young viewers of *Chitty Chitty Bang Bang* were terrified by the nasty Child Catcher employed by the evil Baron Bomburst to snatch and imprison urchins on the streets of Vulgaria.

Cloying See 'Folk Mass' (see p. 86).

Coal bucket Many classrooms, rural and urban, relied for heating on an open fire. Whenever the coal or turf ran low, favoured pupils would be granted a few minutes out of class to fill the coal bucket from the bunker in the schoolyard. On particularly wet or cold days, pupils would take turns to stand by the fire warming or drying themselves two or three at a time.

Concorde While the US and USSR raced for the moon, British and French aviators focused on developing the world's first supersonic passenger aircraft. An Airfix model marked the maiden flight in 1969.

Curry Curry dishes were appearing for the first time in cookbooks and on TV cookery shows. The first curry tasted by most kids came from a Vesta packet.

D

Dave Allen *The Dave Allen Show* was big on the BBC. Irish children allowed to stay up late-ish for one of their parents' favourite shows (it featured countless skits on priests) were fascinated by the ghoulish fun the Dublin comedian made of his missing half-finger.

Dimplex Radiators 'Efficient, economical and perfectly safe for your children.' As Ireland turned on to central heating, Dimplex was the market leader.

Drill The militaristic 1960s name for school PE class. Drill on Telefís Éireann came in the form of *Tone Up*, a twice-weekly four-minute exercise class immediately following the Angelus, targeted at 'all the family, young and old, male and female'. In it: 'Marie O'Sullivan tries the exercises as Commandant J. P. O'Keeffe explains and demonstrates.'

E

Escalator Ireland got its first escalator in early 1963. Installed at Roche's Stores in Dublin's city centre, it became a must-visit carnival ride for small children who insisted their mothers include it on every shopping trip.

Ten talented animals beloved of Sixties children

Basil Brush
Partnered in the 1960s by Mr Rodney (Rodney Bewes) and Mr Derek (Derek Fowlds), Basil was a cultivated fox, modelled on the film star Terry Thomas. A posh puppet who insisted he couldn't stand puppets, Basil was huge by decade's end.

Boris the Stallion
A special bond between girl and horse is formed in the opening episode of *Wild Horses*, set on a Yugoslavian stud farm, after Boris is stolen by fiendish gypsies who dye his white coat brown. Julia leads the rescue mission and a hit series is born.

Cheeta
Ron Ely's comical co-star in the *Tarzan* TV series was played by several chimpanzees in each episode, with the animals assigned scenes depending on what party tricks were called for. Like Skippy and Flipper, Cheeta could make himself understood to humans.

Clarence, The Cross-Eyed Lion
Clarence starred in *Daktari* (meaning 'doctor' in Swahili), an Ivan Tors series that followed the efforts of Dr Marsh Tracy and

his daughter Paula to protect African wildlife from poachers. Judy the chimp doubled as Debbie the Bloop in *Lost In Space*.

Dougal

Such was *The Magic Roundabout*'s popularity with parents that when it was shifted from just before the six o'clock news to an earlier slot in 1967, working adults bombarded the BBC with complaints that their daily home-coming had been ruined. The sugar-lump-loving terrier Dougal was the star.

Flipper

Skippy communicated with his human pal Sonny with a clicking sound, and Flipper, the problem-solving dolphin, used much the same language to warn his young friend Sandy about ship-wrecks, smugglers and killer sharks.

Gentle Ben

Children's TV mogul Ivan Tors adopted the children's book *Gentle Ben* for the small screen, moving the location from Alaska to Florida and switching the bear from brown to black. Gentle Ben's grunts and snarls of chitchat to humans were voiced by a human actor.

Padraig

Padraig, the faithful horse that pulled the Wanderly Wagon through hundreds of opening credits, died of colic shortly after that iconic shoot. There were seven Padraigs during the show's long run, but only one sage old shaggy mutt, Judge.

Petra

Adored by Irish and British children for fifteen years, *Blue Peter*'s first ever pet, Petra the loveable mongrel, was an imposter. The first Petra died of distemper as a tiny puppy two days after her screen debut, and was replaced by a long-lived doppelganger.

Skippy the Bush Kangaroo

The all-action kangaroo had a far higher IQ than the lost hikers and plane-crash survivors he rescued from the parched Australian outback week after week. The Swedes banned the show fearing it would mislead young children into believing marsupials had superpowers.

The vocation of mother-hood and the importance of the family-unit farm

The opening night of Telefís Éireann and the first Saturday-evening schedule

As 7 p.m. approached on the last day of 1961, families, friends and neighbours crowded into parlours and living rooms in party mood to witness the opening night of Telefís Éireann. Arguably more than any other single factor, the coming of television would make the lives of Irish youngsters in the Sixties radically different from that of their parents or, in an age of large families, of their older siblings. On that opening night, however, the new service had no mind to cater for young viewers.

The first speaker on Telefís Éireann was President Éamon de Valera, and he seemed deeply anxious to kill the buzz of excitement coursing through the land. Only eight weeks earlier the planet had teetered on the brink of nuclear war as the United States and the USSR played a terrifying game of chicken during what has become known as The Cuban Missile Crisis. Drawing a parallel with the threat of global extinction, the

President said he was 'afraid' that 'like atomic energy' television could 'do irreparable harm' and 'lead through demoralisation to decadence and disillusion'.

Large swathes of the country missed his keynote speech as viewers frantically tried to adjust their sets to combat patchy signal coverage. Some time before, one expert had submitted a plan to have a special aircraft constantly circling the midlands off which a signal could be bounced to districts with poor or non-existent reception. It was dismissed as daft.

Opening night was initially scheduled for a week earlier, but no one at RTÉ's Montrose headquarters wanted to work on Christmas Day or the days surrounding it, so the big night was put back. The public had been primed with the launch of the  *RTV Guide* (later the *RTÉ Guide*) which had introduced the nation to Nuala Donnelly, Marie O'Sullivan and Kathleen Watkins, the station's continuity announcers, who instantly became Ireland's most glamorous and envied women.

But before the opening-night audience could appreciate any glamour there was the solemn business of blessing the new service to get out of the way. The consecration was duly performed by Dublin's Archbishop John Charles McQuaid. And still it was too early to allow the fun and games begin. Following the benediction, the viewing public were given a virtuous dose of high culture as actors Siobhán McKenna and Micheál MacLiammóir sombrely recited the poetry of Patrick Pearse and W. B. Yeats.

Finally the public got what they wanted as the veteran knockabout comics Jimmy O'Dea and Maureen Potter brought the antics of the music hall into Ireland's living rooms for the first time. The harpist Mary O'Hara, soon to become a nun, was then wheeled on to restore a higher tone.

While the youngsters and most of the nation's adults lapped up the wholesome homespun fare, others watched and waited, half-hoping to see their worst predictions come true. The members of the Catholic Truth Society had been busy for years campaigning to get 'dirty' books banned. In the autumn of 1961, with the start-up of Telefís Éireann now a done deal, the nation's self-appointed mudguards against filth turned their gaze towards the TV screen. One pamphlet told of a woman in England who gave birth in a taxi on the way to hospital because she hadn't been able to drag herself away from her favourite soap.

Irish-language zealots were also deeply worried that the advance of television would wipe out the native tongue through American and British 'colonisation' of our screens.

And although several very senior churchmen commandeered leading on-screen roles on that landmark night, the Catholic bishops still feared for Irish souls. Gathered in Maynooth as the start of the new era loomed, they sent a warning shot across the bows of Montrose, insisting that television 'can do great harm, not only in the diffusion of the ideas of those lacking in deep or accurate knowledge of religious truth, but also in broadcasting programmes which offend all reasonable standards of morals and decency'.

But there was no going back. The bishops and politicians were in broad agreement that Ireland needed its own TV station to rein in viewers tuning in to UTV and the BBC. Some mistrusted the new station's chairman, Eamonn Andrews, who was a huge star in Britain and might be contaminated with un-Irish ideas. The TV sets of the day operated on cathode vacuum tubes which were forever blowing up, and the TV-sceptics were not amused when Andrews jested lamely that Cathleen Ní Houlihan, the symbol of native piety, chastity and virtue, was 'in danger of becoming Cathode Ní Houlihan'. That was precisely what many feared would happen, and to them it was no joking matter.

It was New Year's Eve so children across the country stayed up extra late to enjoy, or endure, footage of the summer visit by Princess Grace, and other big social events of the past year captured on film. The party mood really took over as the cameras showcased the great and the good dancing cheek-to-cheek in their finery at a ritzy Gresham Hotel ball, while the plain people had a singsong in the snow outside. Eamonn Andrews counted down to midnight with the Artane Boys' Band, sportscaster Michael O'Hehir and other luminaries, before Cardinal D'Alton of Armagh brought the merriment to a sombre close with his New Year's address which warned parents not to allow their children to become telly addicts no matter how morally sound the shows might be.

Irish Television's First Saturday Evening Schedule, 6 January 1962

Before the decade had progressed too far, Saturday evenings between the hours of five and nine o'clock would become the golden hours of the week for children's and family shows, showcasing appointment viewing such as *The Monkees, The Man From UNCLE* and *Green Acres.* The first Saturday schedule, however, arguably showed a priority placed on 'improving' young viewers above giving them what they might choose for themselves.

5.00   *Tales Of Wonder.* Emlyn Williams reads *A Child's Christmas* by Dylan Thomas.

5.10   *The Adventures Of Rin Tin Tin.* A boy and his German shepherd dog fight Indians and tame the Wild West.

5.40   *Children's Corner.* With Audrey Meredith. Today, the Cora Cadwell school of Irish dancers.

6.00   *The Angelus*

6.01   *News and Weather*

6.11   *Visitors' Book.* Barry Baker interviews interesting people passing through Ireland this week.

6.45   *The Silent Service.* 'Bergall's Dilemma'. First in a series by Rear Admiral Thomas Dykes about life in the submarine service.

7.15   *For Moderns.* T. P. McKenna introduces a show for moderns of all ages, but particularly those under twenty-five. Includes the week's brightest records, trends in younger fashions and younger newsmakers. Tonight's show features the Ian Henry Jazz Quartet and playwright Kevin Casey.

8.00   *The Twilight Zone*

8.30   *Jackpot.* Gay Byrne presents a new general knowledge quiz game based on an idea by Cecil Sheridan.

Presented first by Gay Byrne and later by Terry Wogan, *Jackpot* was a ratings hit for Telefís Éireann from 1962 to 1965. The Irish show bore a close resemblance to ITV's popular *Criss Cross Quiz* which in turn was a simple variation on noughts & crosses.

Top family films 1961

BABES IN TOYLAND
Starring Annette Funicello

Like Britney Spears, Christina Aguilera and Justin Timberlake long after her, Annette Funicello was a child Mousketeer on Walt Disney's *Mickey Mouse Club*. In this Disney film tailored for the Christmas market, Funicello plays Mary, Mary, Quite Contrary who is about to marry Tom the Piper's Son. The dastardly villain Barnaby hires two goons and instructs them to cast Tom into the sea and steal Mary's sheep, leaving her penniless and alone, and forcing her to consider wedding the scheming Barnaby. Mary is unaware that she is the heir to a fortune, but Barnaby knows that if he marries her he will stand to get his grubby hands on it. The two hired goons sell Tom to the gypsies instead of drowning him, which will prove their undoing, before everything resolves into a happy ending. Paul Anka had a huge hit in 1960 with 'Puppy Love', written about his then girlfriend Funicello.

MYSTERIOUS ISLAND
Starring Michael Craig, Joan Greenwood

Based on Jules Verne's 1874 novel of the same name, this ripping yarn follows the adventures of a group of Union soldiers blown off course as they escape from a Confederate prison camp by hot air balloon. Crashing onto an uncharted island, they come across two Englishwomen shipwrecked by the same storm that brought them there. To their mounting dismay, they discover that the island is home to giant crabs, vicious over-grown birds and monstrous bees, while marauding pirates add to the danger. The future for the visitors seems grim until they are thrown a lifeline by the enigmatic Captain Nemo, who has been observing and helping them from his secret lair.

ONE HUNDRED AND ONE DALMATIANS
Starring Rod Taylor

A year after starring in the all-time sci-fi classic *The Time Machine*, and four years before playing the role of Irish playwright Sean O'Casey in *Young Cassidy*, Hollywood hunk Rod Taylor lent his voice to this animated Disney classic. A huge box-office hit, *One Hundred and One Dalmatians* tells intertwined love stories of a lonesome songwriter called Roger and his faithful hound Pongo (Taylor). Bored with the bachelor life, Pongo decides to find a wife for Roger and a mate for himself. No sooner have Pongo and Perdita produced a litter of adorable offspring than the malevolent Cruella De Vil gatecrashes the party with an evil plot to turn the newborn puppies into a coat for herself. A happy ending gets in her wicked way.

THE PARENT TRAP
Starring Hayley Mills, Maureen O'Hara, Brian Keith

The title song of this hit Disney film was performed by Annette Funicello and Tommy Sands, who were both shooting *Babes In Toyland* at the time. In her second starring role for Disney, child star Hayley Mills plays identical twin sisters Susan Evers and Sharon McKendrick, who have no idea that they are related when they meet at summer camp. As penance for causing chaos they are condemned to suffer each other's company in an 'isolation' cabin, where it dawns that they are twins and that their parents Mitch and Maggie (played by Dubliner Maureen O'Hara) divorced shortly after their birth, taking custody of one child each. The twins, each eager to meet the parent she never knew, switch places. After a series of humorous intrigues, the inevitable happy ending is reached when the girls reunite their warring parents.

VOYAGE TO THE BOTTOM OF THE SEA
Starring Walter Pidgeon, Joan Fontaine, Barbara Eden

Seven years after the US launches the world's first nuclear submarine, the fictional Seaview becomes the cramped setting for a tense drama involving meteor showers, melting ice caps and the possible extinction of life on Earth. The film was co-written and directed by Irwin Allen, who would dominate big-budget children's TV through the 1960s as the mastermind behind hugely successful series including *Lost In Space, Land of the Giants* and *The Time Tunnel.* After shooting finished, the ambitious props were put into storage, so that when Allen decided to make a small screen spin-off, he simply retrieved them and saved a fortune in production costs. In the film, Admiral Nelson and Captain Crane were supported by Lieutenant Cathy Connors played by Barbara Eden who would find children's prime-time fame as the mischievous genie of *I Dream of Jeannie.*

Exposing a broad expanse of abdomen

Dos and don'ts from *The Book Of Courtesy* by Martin Molloy

Published in 1968, Martin Molloy's guide to good behaviour, *The Book Of Courtesy*, sent a message to the youth of Ireland that they should know their place in a highly stratified society, training themselves for the 'rank' they would hold as adults.

The writer urged his young readers to embrace as their motto the words of G. K. Chesterton that: 'Politeness is the Greek word for Patriotism.' Challenging the children of Ireland to live up to their 'noble' Celtic pedigree, he asserted: 'The aristocratic temper of the Irish mind is still very much in evidence.'

DRESS

By 1968 the age of the teenager had well and truly arrived in Ireland, but the writer felt that with a little self-discipline and instruction the genie of teen rebelliousness could be put back in its bottle.

He declared: 'Despite the rarity and eccentricity of modern youths' fashions it is a mark of the mature and balanced person that he does not follow every fad and refuses to be exploited by commercialism.'

While girls' communion and confirmation dresses were generally put carefully away for the next in line after a few wears, a boy's confirmation suit became his Sunday best until he grew out of it, to be worn for the countless parades and holy days that peppered the calendar. The writer recommended that: 'The *Fáinne Nua* looks better in the tie than on the lapel.'

The lapel pin called the *Fáinne* indicated that the wearer had some fluency in the Irish language. There were three grades of *Fáinne* (meaning ring or circle). The Republican activist Piaras Béaslaí had introduced the scheme in 1911. The first wave of enthusiasm for the *Fáinne* faded badly, not least because impoverished native speakers couldn't afford them, but by the start of the 1960s, along with *báinín* sweaters, rousing folk ballads and bushy beards, the pins were part of a fad for all things that proudly proclaimed the Irish free spirit. In a decade when Ireland's kids started to wear *Man From UNCLE* secret agent badges and bangles that came as free gifts with *Bunty* and *Judy*, the *Fáinne Nua* was one of the few childhood fashion accessories that had the approval of parents, teachers and clerics.

IN THE STREET

According to Martin Molloy: 'The most obvious rule, of course, is that a gentleman, when accompanying a lady, always walks

on the outside. The same rule applies when accompanying an elderly person, male or female, a clergy-man or a person of higher rank.'

The writer insisted that: 'Eating apples, oranges, ice-cream etc. in the street or at public gatherings is a liberty permitted only to small children. Whistling, at all times, is a messenger boy habit.'

OCCUPYING A CHAIR

In a great many homes, urban and rural, the best-kept room was referred to as 'the parlour', and was reserved for entertaining guests and receiving important callers such as the parish priest, the schoolteacher or the insurance salesman.

On the rare occasions children were allowed into the parlour, it was as visitors to a part of their home that was normally off limits. The writer warned: 'Using a chair is a very simple act and yet by ordinary standards it admits of fifteen different ways in which one can offend against good manners. Lounging in a chair is disrespectful to others present, especially when it results in exposing a broad expanse of abdomen.'

Child's play

The lexicon of bouncing balls

Many of the ball-against-the wall games popular with Sixties children had their origins decades earlier in the 'hard areas' of Ireland's semi-industrialised towns and cities. Hard, flat footpaths, roads and gable walls made good bouncing surfaces for rubber balls. While the popularity of these games has plunged in the hi-tech twenty-first century, they still provide a fun way for growing kids from Malin to Mizen to sharpen their motor skills.

Experts who have studied these children's games have concluded that, far from being rhyming gibberish, the verses that accompany them – such as 'One, Two, Three O'Leary' and 'Queenie-i-o, Who's Got The Ball' – have an inbuilt rhythmic coded language that issues quick-fire instructions for the players. The participants must strictly follow the mosaic of rules, rhythms and rhymes in a test of skill, coordination and concentration. Certain trigger words demand an instant response that produces a gear-shift in the game.

Despite the fact that these ball games are never formally taught, but passed on orally from child to child, the basic moves and terms are virtually identical in every part of the country. The most common actions, and their surprisingly universal names, are:

Plainy: The most basic move of all. The ball is thrown straight at the wall and caught on the rebound. No embellishments.

Rolley: The player rolls their hands, disco-dancing style, while the ball is in flight.

Clappy: The player claps hands while awaiting the rebound.

Backey: The player claps hands behind their back before catching the return.

Tippy: The player tips the ground before catching the rebound.

Hippy: The player tips their hips while the ball is in flight.

Burl Around: The player whirls completely around after throwing.

Jelly Bag: The player cups both hands together to form a 'bag' for catching the ball.

Over: Bowl the ball overarm as in cricket.

Basket: The player locks the fingers into a reverse bag with the knuckles facing into their chest, making the catch a tricky manoeuvre.

Dropsie/Downie: The ball must bounce off the ground before it is caught.

Bouncie/Dizzie/Dashy: The ball is bounced off the ground before it hits the wall.

Right Leg/Left Leg: The ball is launched under a raised leg, usually aimed to hit the ground before bouncing back off the wall.

Backy: The player stands sideways to the wall, throwing the ball from behind their back to bounce off the ground and then the wall.

Upsie: Do the required move, but with the ball making contact higher up the wall.

Winning two world wars, having an empire and generally being great

The British comics beloved of 1960s Irish kids

As had been the case for generations, the comics treasured by Irish children of the 1960s were British through and through. Besides promoting the virtues of honesty, patience and manners, they also trumpeted the innate superiority of the British character, the heroism of the British Armed Forces, and the world-beating spirit of the England football team – but all of that was by the by to legions of Irish readers whose only concern was what manner of mischief Dennis the Menace or Keyhole Kate would get up to this time.

The decade began during the first age of the teenage tearaway or, in the parlance of the time, the juvenile delinquent.

Teenagers seldom darkened the pages of the weekly comics populated by young boys from some place that was forever the 1930s in short trousers with a sling poking from their back pocket, and impish tomboys in pigtails. There were bullies, lots of them, but they were guaranteed a comeuppance, often in the form of a good spanking with a father's slipper or a caning by the teacher.

D. C. Thompson, which produced just about every British comic of note during the twentieth century, was founded in Dundee in 1905 with a strict no-unions and no-Catholics employment policy. Despite their Scottish roots, the comics came to inhabit a place that seemed forever a little part of England and indeed, an enduring part of Little England. Welsh characters were called 'Taffy'. Scots folk said 'hoots' and hankered for haggis. The dusky-skinned Sparky, from further afield, wore a grass skirt and a bone through his nose. Little Plum (Your Redskin Chum), came from the Smellyfeet tribe and said 'pass um salt' instead of 'pass the salt'. Even in a universe of magic shoes (Billy's Boots), rogue robots (Tin Lizzie) and crime-solving border collies (Black Bob), Englishness was the benchmark of normality.

As a kid in Ireland, this seemed the natural order of things. British comics were a treasured splash of colour in a world devoid of PlayStations and 3D big screen blockbusters, so when Roy of the Rovers taught you that all foreign footballers were dirty cheats with spiv moustaches, that was simply the way of the world. Roy Race, the most decorated player in history, was also the most kidnapped, finding himself held to ransom several times while his team Melchester Rovers visited dodgy Latin American tinpot dictatorships.

The Victor's Tough of the Track, Alf Tupper, merged English sporting superiority with another obsession of the comics, food. A welder who lived on fish and chips wrapped in newspaper, Alf would routinely arrive at a big athletics tournament in the nick of time to win a big race, having been sidetracked rescuing a kitten or evading yet more kidnappers.

When summer holidays came, the first and most important stop on the long drive to wherever the average Irish family was bound was to pick up Roy, Alf, Dennis the Menace, The Four Marys and all their chums. Together they shortened the journey and, after the family had bedded in, helped pass the long hours of close confinement as monsoons engulfed the caravan parks of Ballybunion and Bundoran.

But back to the food fixation. Wartime food rationing in Britain outlasted the Second World War by fully nine years and did not end until 1954. It had an even longer afterlife in the comics, lasting well into the 1970s. For *Bunty*'s cover stars, The Four Marys, there was nothing yummier or scrummier than a midnight feast in the dorm of their posh boarding school. For *Beano*'s rougher Bash Street Kids it was mince pies and wine gums. *Dandy*'s Desperate Dan ate huge cow pies with the horns sticking out. *Sparky*'s Hungry Horace simply hoovered up food.

While the comics fuelled flights of fantasy in young readers, they tended to be arch-conservative on just about everything else until many were given a long belated makeover in the 1980s. As The Beatles and Carnaby Street swept the globe, the comics virtually blanked the Swinging Sixties in favour of old certainties like winning two world wars, having an empire and generally being great. Any references to the pop and fashion of the day tended to lampoon both. Boys and girls just wanted to have fun, long-suffering fathers always wore cardigans, had moustaches and smoked pipes, and the cartoon parents of young children invariably looked like they were ready for packing off to the old folks home. The one nod to the modern world, inevitably, was to England's hosting of the football World Cup in 1966. For comic readers, the World Cup Finals held in England in the summer of 1966 actually lasted eight years, made up of the four years of build-up before the event, the tournament itself, and the four-year build-up to the 1970 competition, since as reigning world champions, England had pre-qualified to be there.

The English jingoism dripping off the pages of the imported comics was a matter of blissful indifference to every young child in Ireland who eagerly awaited them every Thursday or Friday. There were times, however, when the comics made the Irish reader desperately wish they were English. These agonising occasions were when they contained a free gift or a special offer.

The first issue of *Hotspur*, for instance, contained a free mask and an offer for an 'electric shock' prank device. The first *Mandy* gave away 'a lovely rainbow ring', unless you lived in Ireland. Sometimes the free gifts didn't even cross the sea to the Northern Ireland part of the United Kingdom. Balsa wood glider aircraft were a popular giveaway, along with cardboard dolls and cut-out frocks, glossy cardboard spy decoders and other lightweight gifts.

These special editions were a source of deep childhood trauma for countless Irish kids, as they read the chilling words: 'Offer does not apply in Eire.'

Young hearts sank across Ireland as the nation's children learnt the true meaning of the term 'read 'em and weep'.

TEN CHERISHED COMICS OF 1960s IRELAND

The Beano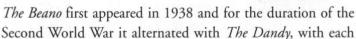

The Beano first appeared in 1938 and for the duration of the Second World War it alternated with *The Dandy*, with each appearing once every fortnight due to paper and ink rationing. By the start of the 1960s *The Beano* featured a stable line-up of iconic characters led by Roger the Dodger, Dennis the Menace, Minnie the Minx, Little Plum, The Three Bears, Billy Whizz and The Bash Street Kids. The Kids of Class 11B were led by Danny, who could always be relied on to tough it out in a crisis, and if there wasn't a crisis he'd create one. The goonish Plug had a face not even a mother could love, Erbert was blind as a bat while Smiffy was thicker than several short planks. While Dennis the Menace and Roger the Dodger may have looked quite similar, the former was a serial troublemaker while Roger devoted his energies to conserving energy, skiving out of chores and homework, and avoiding the clutches of his tormentor, the bully Cruncher Kerr.

The Beezer and Topper

Both born in the 1950s, these sister comics reached their peak popularity in the 1960s before a long decline set in, resulting in their eventual merger in 1990 as *The Beezer and Topper*. Both were printed in an A3 format, making them the size of broadsheet newspapers rather than regular comics. The undoubted star of *The Topper* was Beryl the Peril, created by cartoonist David Law as a counterpart to his own Dennis the Menace from *The Beano*. Dressed in the same red-and-black livery as Dennis, Beryl's mission in life was to terrorise her teachers, neighbours and parents, who bore a suspiciously close similarity to Dennis' long-suffering folks. *The Beezer*'s main attractions included Calamity Jane, an accident waiting to happen every time, and Pop, Dick and Harry, in which terrible twins Dick and Harry thought up fresh tortures for their portly Dad Pop every week. Nosey Parker, meanwhile, was a schoolboy whose elastic, extendable nose got him into all sorts of mischief.

Bunty

Two years old at the start of the decade, *Bunty* was a firm favourite with Irish girls. The average issue featured several short comic-strip stories, letters pages, competitions, puzzles, promotions and advertisements. The back page throughout the 1960s featured a cut-out doll with changeable clothes. Cover stars The Four Marys were Mary Field, Mary Cotter, Mary Simpson and Mary Radleigh, aka Fieldy, Cotty, Simpy and Raddy. They were all in the Third Form at St Elmo's School for Girls in Elmbury and, like The Beatles, each reader tended to have their personal favourite Mary. The foursome were forever pitting their wits against the class snobs Mabel and Veronica, who especially picked on Simpy because she was a scholarship girl from a working-class background. The girls' activities during the 1960s included helping teachers with their amnesia so they could claim their rightful inheritance, getting domestic servants out of scrapes, and punishing exam cheats.

The Dandy

Throughout the 1960s the featured strip on the cover of *The Dandy* was always Korgy the Cat, an accident-prone black feline, but the character best known to the general public was Desperate Dan. The barrel-chested cowboy strongman was able to lift a cow over his head with one hand, and his stubble was so rough that he shaved using a blowtorch. Another veteran of Issue One in 1937 who remained popular through the 1960s was Keyhole Kate, a lippy young girl with a compulsive-obsessive disorder for spying through people's keyholes. In an era when robots on the big and small screen were invariably blocky, metallic and death-dealing, Brassneck provided a neat parody in the form of a painfully thin android nailed together in woodwork class and dressed in an ill-fitting school uniform. The characters would frequently trespass across the pages into each other's strips, which was made possible by the fact that they were all neighbours in Dandytown.

The Eagle

The Eagle began the 1960s flying high but ended the decade being subsumed into its arch-rival *Lion* in 1969. Founded by Anglican vicar Marcus Morris, the comic set itself the task of edifying young readers as well as entertaining them. *The Eagle* was to provide a Christian alternative to the US comics that were becoming popular with young boys, which Morris denounced as 'deplorable, nastily over-violent and obscene, often with undue emphasis on the supernatural and magical as a way of solving problems'. Unlike its rivals, *The Eagle* contained sections devoted to news and sports coverage, as well as educational cutaway diagrams of complex machinery. The cover star of *The Eagle* from the outset was the square-jawed space hero Dan Dare, Pilot of the Future. Each week Dare would pit his warrior skills against his arch-enemy, The Mekon of Meknota, a hyper-intelligent creature with an oversized brain perched atop a puny body. The vicar parted company with his comic on the cusp of the 1960s and the falling standards which followed his jumping ship were reflected in dwindling sales.

Judy

Judy's popular strips of the 1960s included Bobtail the Beach Rescue, Sally of Studio Seven and Boomerang, The Horse That Always Comes Back, but the star of the show from her first appearance in 1968 was Bobby Dazzler. Roberta Dazzler – Bobby to her friends – was the only girl at Westbury Boarding School for Boys thanks to the fact that her mother had landed the job of matron. Mike Norton and the other third formers devote a great deal of effort, in the form of pranks and other trickery, to prove beyond a doubt that boys are smarter than girls. Their various backfiring escapades include presenting Bobby with a doll and pram for her birthday, trying to scare her with spiders and generally trying to exploit every gender stereotype in the book. Invariably, by the end of each storyline Bobby has demonstrated that girls are better than boys, and the lads get some manner of embarrassing comeuppance.

Look and Learn

First published in 1962 *Look and Learn* was the comic that met with the highest approval ratings from parents, as it put education at the top of its agenda. Regular original features included Asterix and the sci-fi serial 'The Rise of the Trigan Empire', but they shared the pages with classic works of literature retold in comic strip form including *Lorna Doone* and

H. G. Wells' *The First Men In The Moon*. Launched at a time when the moon race had begun in earnest, *Look and Learn* featured regular reports on new developments in space travel. Non-comic-strip features covered such topics as The Grand Canyon, The Quest For Oil, The Story Of A Seed and the activities of the World Wildlife Fund. One of *Look and Learn's* most popular features was its Pen Friends section which encouraged young readers to make long-distance friendships by airmail.

Mandy

One of the prime directives of the *Mandy* writers appeared to be to nudge young girls into considering a job in one of the caring professions, such as nursing, or working with small children or animals. However, the young women in the stories rarely aspired to become a doctor or a vet, but to provide the best support a girl could give to the men in those roles. The recurring themes of the comic strips included orphans suffering mistreatment at the hands of cruel relatives, girls trying to shake off a gypsy curse, bad girls faking some disability or other to take advantage of kind souls, and girls enduring blackmail or hardship in order to protect some family secret. Two of the most popular and enduring characters were Valda and Angel. Valda was a time traveller who drew her remarkable powers from a Crystal of Life that was always getting lost or stolen. Her mission was to come to the aid of those in difficulty. Angel was a young girl who, discovering that she had only a year to live, devotes her remaining time to helping the waifs of Victorian London.

Sparky

From its launch in 1965 until the close of the decade, the cover star of *Sparky* comic was Sparky himself, and white Irish kids would have been largely oblivious to the fact that the character and the storylines were deeply non-PC. Sparky was a black boy living in an all-white English town. His entire wardrobe consisted of a grass skirt and a couple of baubles. While all the other characters were drawn in normal proportions, Sparky's body was distended while his lips were preposterously thick and red. In fact, Sparky was a blatant revival of Sooty Snowball, a racist caricature from the 1930s publication *Magic Comic*. Keyhole Kate and Hungry Horace migrated to *Sparky* from *The Dandy*, and Nosey Parker from *The Beezer*. One of the most popular strips was Lonely Wood, which followed the animal rescue escapades of brother and sister Frank and Pat Freeman who, week after week, would come across injured or lost animals in urgent need of tender loving care.

The Tiger

In the aftermath of a couple of 1960s mergers, the comic had spells as *Tiger & Hurricane* and *Tiger & Jag*, but as *Tiger* it was home to the adventures of Jim 'Jet Ace' Logan, Roy of the Rovers and Billy's Boots. The intrepid Logan was a space pilot with the 21st-century RAF, battling evil aliens and ecological ruin. Schoolboy Billy Dane was a rubbish footballer until he tried on the boots of his gifted grandfather Dead Shot Keen. The old boots transformed young Billy into a world-class striker, but every week he'd either lose them or have them stolen. Roy Race, aka Roy of the Rovers, faced similar traumas at regular intervals. The king of the dramatic last-gasp winner, Race was kidnapped on more than one occasion and was even the victim of a mystery shooting that failed to keep him on the treatment couch for too long. The strip followed the structure of the actual English football season, which meant a long summer break. So for most 1960s summers, the storyline involved Melchester United touring some lawless expanse of jungle where all manner of shady foreigners plotted bad things.

Lessons in talking proper

Parents, teachers and priests have a patriotic obligation to help

One of the most obvious and immediate threats presented by the invasion of pop culture and television was to the way children spoke. From 'fab' to 'far out', 'groovy' to 'hassle', and from 'vibes' to 'rip off', the slang of foreign mean streets was

 flooding the country, cruelly infecting, worst of all, the youngest and most suggestible. Many middle-class parents did the best they could for their children by enrolling them for extracurricular elocution lessons in how to talk proper.

Martin Molloy, in his 1968 *Book of Courtesy*, addressed the issue in a section entitled 'Mode of Speech'. For Molloy, the first task of the elocution teacher was to sort out problems dating back much farther than the recent advent of the teenage tearaway and his scruffy hippy cousin.

Advising parents and pupils that they must present a well-balanced public persona, Molloy suggested: 'Be wary of adopting a "grawnd" accent because of its association with the foreigner and the Ascendancy. It is regarded with some suspicion, notwithstanding the fact that some of Ireland's greatest patriots spoke this way. A "refayned" accent is sometimes considered un-Irish and, in extremes of interpretation, even indicative of faintly "traitorous" leanings.'

He continued: 'At the other end of the scale are the Paddy Whacks whose concept of being truly Irish consists of speaking in a crudely exaggerated and entirely personal brand of parish pump accent. It is an unworthy relic of enforced illiteracy.'

And finally: 'Bad pronunciation – "dis" and "dat" instead of this and that; bad grammar; "he go" instead of "he goes", "I seen" for "I saw"; these must be recognised for what they really are, a survival from our days of deprivation. Parents, teachers and priests have a patriotic obligation to help in eliminating this unworthy brand of servitude.'

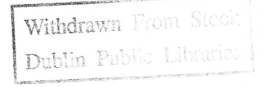

A–Z

F

Folk Mass Invariably featuring an ardent rendition of 'Morning Has Broken', the Folk Mass first appeared in the United States in the late 1960s and quickly migrated to Ireland. Its rowdy, boozy adult counterpart was the All Priests' travelling cabaret show fronted by the self-styled 'Mod Priest' Father Michael Cleary. The All Priests Shows provided clerical blessing for groups of housewives to enjoy a night out and a few drinks in an era when such behaviour was widely frowned upon – by men.

'Foreign' Games In 1967 Education Minister Donogh O'Malley expressed regret at a Shannon Rugby Club dinner that he had no control over schools that banned 'foreign' games. He remarked: 'I think the pupils should be consulted on their choice of sports. Rugby and soccer people as well as others are sick and tired of having the finger pointed at us as if we were any worse Irishmen for playing these games.'

G

Galloping Gourmet Pitched as the James Bond of the cookery set with his suave manner and matinee-idol looks, debonair Graham Kerr scored a huge TV hit as the Galloping Gourmet. Apparently licensed to kill, he pumped, squeezed, squashed and syphoned lashings of butter and cream into every dish that would take it.

General election Kids were deprived of their TV fix on the day of the count for the 1965 general election when RTÉ suspended its entire schedule to run a television special. The station borrowed a state-of-the-art computer from Bord na Móna to crunch the numbers pouring in from around the constituencies. The data spewing out of the space age computer was then chalked up on school blackboards in the studio.

Generation Gap Defined as 'a lack of communication between one generation and another, especially between young people and their parents, brought about by differences of tastes, values, outlook, etc.', the gap yawned to a chasm in the 1960s.

The Ghost and Mrs Muir The ghost in this popular US sitcom was, according to his PR people, 'handsome 6'3" Corkman' Edward Mulhare.

Green Shield Stamps A British adaptation of the trading stamps popular in the US, Green Shield stamps were handed out with purchases of groceries and petrol, to be stuck like sheets of postage stamps into a collector's book. Full books were exchanged for goods from the Green Shield Catalogue.

Guinea One pound and one shilling, or twenty-one shillings. Parents taking their sick child to the doctor might be charged in guineas. Auctioneers, lawyers and other professionals would quote fees in guineas, though the guinea coin itself had long vanished as legal tender.

Guinness Book of Records First published in 1955 following a dispute between members of a wildfowl shooting party in Wexford, this was amongst the best-selling Christmas gifts every year of the decade. The story goes that in 1951 the managing director of Guinness, Sir Hugh Beaver, was shooting on the marshy North Slob of the Slaney River in County Wexford. After missing a shot at a golden plover, Beaver became involved in an argument over which was Europe's fastest game bird, the breed he'd just missed or the red grouse. According to the first *Guinness Book of Records*, the correct answer was the bird that bested Beaver.

Top family films 1962

DR NO
Starring Sean Connery, Ursula Andress, Joseph Wiseman

The 007 franchise hit the ground running with this hard-boiled interpretation of Ian Fleming's 1958 novel. It introduced Sean Connery as the planet's least secretive secret agent, and the evil empire of SPECTRE, which would become a recurring feature of the Bond films. Connery reputedly only landed the role after Cary Grant and Leitrim's Patrick McGoohan both refused to commit. *Time* heaped scorn on Connery's character, calling his 'silly' Bond 'a blithering bounder' and a 'great big hairy marshmallow'. The Vatican condemned *Dr No* for its cruelty and lewdness, while the Kremlin derided the hero as a symbol of everything that was evil about capitalism. Hugely successful at the box office, *Dr No* was also hugely influential, inspiring a host of both big- and small-screen imitators.

JACK THE GIANT KILLER
Starring Kerwin Mathews

Upon the release of this stop-motion animation film, critics pointed out that many of its monsters bore a close resemblance to the banshees that featured in the 1959 children's hit *Darby O'Gill and The Little People* starring Sean Connery. The traditional tale of the plucky young man who defends a princess from giants and demons has historical roots in the Irish myths of Finn mac Cumhail. The debt to Irish folklore was repaid in a plot line which involves the intrepid Jack recruiting the magical services of Diaboltin, a leprechaun imprisoned in a bottle by the King of the Elves for the crime of crafting seven-league boots from his crock of gold. After a series of wild and often violent adventures, Jack frees the leprechaun from his bottle. Diaboltin uses his boots to return to Ireland while guiding Jack and the rest of his heroic band home to Britain.

MR HOBBS TAKES A VACATION
Starring James Stewart, Maureen O'Hara

Stewart plays Roger Hobbs, a burnt-out banker whose wife Peggy (O'Hara) plans a quiet seaside holiday with their growing children, young grandchildren and family cook. The holiday location turns out to be anything but restful and tensions boil up as various social and generation gaps emerge to threaten every prospect of peace ever breaking out. One by one, the canny Roger and Peggy apply themselves to the task of peace-making. Stewart's character bonds with his teenage son Danny on a boating trip, and escorts his youngest daughter Katey to a hop at the yacht club, where future Sixties music star Herb Alpert (the A in A&M Records) is the resident trumpet player. This warm and fuzzy family romp was a big international hit, and launched Stewart in a series of similar roles.

THE MUSIC MAN
Starring Robert Preston, Shirley Jones, Paul Ford

This feel-good film taken from the hit Broadway musical of the same name was one of the biggest international box-office draws of the early Sixties, while providing Irish radio with one of its most-played children's favourites in the form of 'Seventy-Six Trombones'. Played by Robert Preston, the villain who turns out to have a heart of gold is Harry Hill, who sets out to swindle the parents of a small Iowa city, and ends up creating the best boys' marching band in America while also getting the girl, played by Shirley Jones. Already the established star of *Oklahoma!* and *Carousel*, Jones would become a top name of 1970s children's TV as the protective mother of *The Partridge Family* which featured her real-life heartthrob stepson David Cassidy.

THE WONDERFUL WORLD OF THE BROTHERS GRIMM

Starring Lawrence Harvey, Claire Bloom, Barbara Eden

This fantasy film was a big hit across Ireland despite the fact that its special effects were largely lost on Irish audiences. Shot from three camera angles in a process known as Cinerama, it was seen to best panoramic effect in a large theatre with the images from three projectors beamed onto a screen curving 146 degrees. After working their way through a compelling series of fairy-tales, the Grimm brothers Wilhelm and Jacob find deserved acclaim. At the close of the film, as their train pulls into the station, a crowd of children storm onto the platform demanding: 'We want a story!' Wilhelm tells them: 'Once upon a time there were two brothers ...' As the children cheer, the film ends with the caption: '... and they lived happily ever after'.

The Sunday drive

The coming of the family car and the ice-cream van

The motorised family day at the seaside had been a feature of Irish life for a whole century by the start of the 1960s. The Wicklow town of Bray, for instance, had been a magnet for day trippers from the capital ever since a rail link to Dublin was opened in the 1850s. Trams, charabancs and the country's biggest mass transport system, the bicycle, had since opened up the east coast, the countryside and the mountains to picnickers, but it was the huge increase in car ownership from the start of the 1960s that put the nation's beauty spots within quick and easy reach.

Not everyone was happy with this new weekly invasion of proud first-time car owners blotting the landscape with their mewling children, frisky hounds and Primus stoves. And wherever these day-tripping menageries went, the new phenomenon of the ice-cream van was sure to follow, its wobbly out-of-tune chimes driving parents and kids to distraction, although for different reasons.

In Belfast, Alderman Gerry Fitt denounced these noisy four-wheeled vending machines as dangerous 'pied pipers', luring frenzied children to run excitedly onto busy roadways. Fitt demanded that if ice-cream vans were to be tolerated, every driver should have a helper who would guard the children while they milled about.

In Dublin the city fathers summonsed a number of motor-ised ice-cream vendors under various bye-laws, only for the judges to throw out the cases. Taking their cue from Northern Ireland, local authorities in the south managed to impose a ban on the hurdy-gurdy chimes at some beauty spots, but this did nothing to curb business, much to the annoyance of those, often well-heeled, objectors who'd had the beauty spots to themselves up until now and greatly resented the intrusion of the great unwashed and the parasitical ice-cream vendors who lowered the tone even further.

One *Irish Times* contributor griped in 1964: 'Have you been up the Dublin Mountains recently of a weekend? A few years ago you could drive the family up Glencree and around the Pine Forest county and you could be pardoned for being annoyed if you met two dozen cars of an afternoon. Last Sunday the roadsides were jammed with cars and it is as hard to get parking space as if it were O'Connell Street on a busy weekday. A sign of the times is that the mobile ice cream vans are now finding it very profitable indeed to "go up the mountains" at weekends where, without any jingles to advertise their presence, they do enough business to make the operation profitable.'

The same complainant muttered that the new mass owner-ship of cars was also ruining Ireland's beaches with 'the shrilling of children and screeching of transistorised Beatles'. Another wrote in to concur, saying that pesky car owners with their squawking gaggles of children were turning the north Dublin resort of Skerries into a honky-tonk joint made up of 'gaudy multi-coloured kiosks with their jukeboxes, coffee dispensers, slot machines and an abundance of litter'. The writer was deeply annoyed that 'the chiming ice cream van plying its wares will benefit most' from this child-centred vandalism.

A–Z

H

Heart Transplant This new procedure was constantly in the news from the first failed attempt to put a chimp's heart into a human in 1964 to the first successful operation by Dr Christiaan Barnard in 1967, although the recipient survived just eighteen days.

Hopscotch For a great many boys and girls, the best use ever found for classroom chalk was to mark out the lines of a hopscotch court in the school playground. The grids were generally refreshed each day, and as the state began replacing crumbling Victorian infrastructures with pop-up prefabs, the newly laid black tarmac playgrounds showed up the hopscotch court better than ever before. The game may be an English import to Ireland, and according to a 1707 edition of *Poor Robin's Almanac* it was not the sole preserve of small children. According to that publication, which had first mentioned the game forty years earlier, 'Lawyers and Physicians have little to do this month, so they may (if they will) play at Scotch-hoppers.'

    With regional variations, the rules have remained much the same down the centuries, with the first player tossing or kicking the marker into the first square. Today any number of objects serve as markers, but in the 1960s the marker was usually a flattish stone or a tin of shoe polish. The marker must land completely within the designated square and without touching a line or bouncing out. The player then hops through the course, skipping the square with the marker in it. Single squares must be hopped on one foot. For the first single square, either foot may be used. Side by side squares are straddled, with the left foot landing in the left square, and the right foot landing in the right square. Optional squares marked Safe, Home, or Rest are neutral squares, and may be hopped through in any manner without penalty. After landing in the end, safe, square, the player must turn around and return through the course. They then must retrieve their marker and continue the course as stated without touching a line or stepping into a square with another player's marker. If the player steps on a line, misses a square, or falls over, the turn ends. Players begin their turns where they last left off. The first player to complete one course for every numbered square on the court wins the game.

Horse Show The annual Dublin Horse Show at the RDS was one of the sporting highlights of each year, attracting blanket media coverage. In 1968 almost the entire front page of the *Irish Independent* was cleared of news and given over to the question framed in the banner headline: 'Can We Hold Aga Khan Trophy?' English showjumper Harvey Smith, famous for his 'two-fingered salutes', was the people's champion.

Hovercraft Late in the decade this hovering seacraft went into commercial service between England and France. British TV, newspapers and kids' comics went to town on it and every small boy wanted to drive one.

I

The Iceberger Launched by HB in 1968, the Ice-berger seemed a novel departure to a young generation, but in fact the ice-cream sandwich was a creation that dated back to the start of the century.

Instant Camera

Launched in 1965 with its disposable single flash bulbs, the Kodak Polaroid Model 20 Swinger was the hip gadget for capturing the action at parties and outings.

Isolationism Ireland's long, failed protectionist policy of economic self-sufficiency was abandoned at the start of the decade by new Taoiseach Seán Lemass who reversed measures he himself had introduced thirty years earlier. The lowering of trade barriers opened the way for more imported toys, sweets and other treats.

She may become beauty editor of a fashion magazine

Irish children were conditioned to think small about their futures

'For daughters, jobs where beauty and appearance are important count the most.'
– *Sunday Review*, February 1963

For most of the 1960s Irish children could legally leave school and enter the adult workforce at the age of fourteen. In practice, many thousands left full-time education earlier. Certain that they were going to quit the system the day they turned fourteen, a large number of rural pupils never bothered making the transition to secondary school. Instead, with the cooperation of teachers, they sat in on primary classes until their fourteenth birthday arrived. In 1965 an investigative panel commissioned by the government reported that of those fourteen-year-olds leaving education in 1962–63, just over one in four had completed their Primary Certificate, which indicated they could muster some basic level of reading, writing and numeracy.

Irish society throughout the decade remained highly stratified. To a great extent, farmers' sons became farmers, plumbers' sons became plumbers and the sons of the professions went into one of the professions. A permanent and pensionable job in the civil service was the ambition of almost every middle-class parent for their offspring. The career prospects of the nations' daughters was a matter of some indifference. Girls could join the civil service straight from school on the lowest rung of the ladder, that of Clerical Assistant. Boys who gained entry to that bureaucracy started at the higher-paid grade of Clerical Officer. Women had to quit their civil service jobs as soon as they wed, under the State's marriage bar. The countless young males who reached the age of eighteen without a job could automatically sign on the dole, but there was no such provision for girls.

Many of the girls who left school in their mid-teens found that, if they didn't take the boat, their job options ran little further than becoming dispensable production-line fodder for the country's manufacturing industries which were putting on a minor spurt. In 1965 the management of a Dublin ice-cream factory served a typically stern notice on the exclusively female staff who must have felt that they'd never really escaped the confinements of school.

It instructed that each girl must put in a full forty-two and a half hours per week at their work station, clocking in by 8.04 a.m. and not moving from that spot without permission of a supervisor. Any girl clocking in between 8.04 a.m. and 8.10 a.m. would be permitted to start work, but would be docked one hour's pay. Anyone arriving after that would be sent home and readmitted at 2 p.m. at a loss of five hours' pay. Nail varnish, hair rollers and jewellery were all forbidden. At the end of a long list of dos and don'ts, each girl was reminded to 'put her house in order' or sterner discipline would be imposed.

This harsh workplace reality was very different from the soft-focus possible futures being peddled by the *Encyclopaedia Britannica* in its children's editions which were to be found in countless Irish households. It was the era of the door-to-door encyclopaedia salesman, and many Irish parents invested in instalments in their kiddies' future, often signing up for supplementary series such as *Britannica*'s glossy *Advisory Guides For Parents*.

Published in 1965, one of these parental guides was entitled *Preparing A Children's Party*. The guidelines for one of the suggested themed celebrations was for:

A Careers Party For Ages 7–9.

Space: Big room or garden.

Invitations: 'What do you want to be when you grow up? Come to my party dressed for your future job and tell us all about it.'

Party: Guests arrive dressed as nurses, doctors, lawyers, mothers, ballet dancers, pop singers etc. Start party off with a game of Impersonations (the child writes down the name of the well-known person they're going to impersonate and the winner is the first to guess the person). Partner children and let them work out in pairs what they will reply to a fast-moving Twenty Questions about their chosen career.

> **Food**: Children in this age group are still suspicious of unknown mixtures in sandwiches. Keep ingredients separate: tomato, egg, cream cheese or ham. Flapjacks, macaroons, three-colour sponge. Orangeade.

Towards the end of the decade the Irish government produced some 200 information brochures of its own, providing career guidance available to boys and girls entering secondary school at the age of twelve. Overwhelmingly, the thrust of the state initiative was to prepare the boys and girls of Ireland for a job for life, or, in the case of the girls, for a job until they got married and settled down to keep house and raise kids.

While the children of *Encyclopaedia Britannica* subscribers were being encouraged to give at least a flighty thought to becoming a ballet dancer or a pop singer, the attainable jobs advocated by the Irish state were grounded in the real worlds of manual labour, the trades, and the civil service. While the professions were equal-opportunities employers in theory at least, most of the state-approved future careers were open to males only, while the slim choices labelled 'Girls Only' included Beautician, Waitress, Hotel Receptionist, Air/Ground Hostess with Aer Lingus, Inspector of Poultry-Keeping and Butter-Making, and Fashion Model.

Boys engaging with the school career-guidance teacher would be pointed at some very specific state-backed jobs, such as Ship's Steward and Ship's Cook in Irish Shipping Ltd, Station Assistant with the Meteorological Service,

Postman, Airline Pilot, and Male Night Telephonist with the Department of Post & Telegraphs. All of these were marked 'Boys Only' on the official pamphlets. While the job of telephonist was generally thought very suitable for girls, it was not deemed proper that they should work nights in proximity to male colleagues.

State-approved careers marked open to 'Boys And Girls' included Interviewer/Reporter with Raidió Teilifís Éireann, Third Secretary in the Department of Foreign Affairs, Occupational Therapist Treating Mental and Physical Illness, Instructor in Horticulture and Bee Keeping, Hairdresser, Dress Designer and Teacher of Hearing Impaired Children.

But before a child could take Step One on the path to a career, they had to give some thought to the obstacles and expectations placed in their way by a deeply conservative, deeply stratified society. For girls in particular, the list of Terms & Conditions was long, onerous and almost certainly drawn up by a committee of middle-aged men. Girls could look forward to earning substantially less than boys for doing the same work. On the first day of 1960 twelve women were training to become Ireland's first female police officers. Women officers at the end of the decade earned a weekly wage of £11-2-9 while their male counterparts received £12-17-6 for identical duties. Despite the fact that only a very small minority of the population could speak or understand Irish, applicants for even the most menial state-affiliated jobs were supposed to display a functioning grasp of the language.

Instructor in poultry-keeping & butter-making. Girls only.
'She is expected to develop local leadership and to cultivate an

energetic and intelligent approach among the farming community towards improving, through cooperative effort, the economic and social conditions of their areas ... The position is pensionable but instructors are required to resign on marriage.'

Bus Conductor with Coras Iompair Éireann. Boys only.

'Must be at least five foot five inches in stockinged feet ... Duties include collecting fares and issuing tickets to passengers, signalling the driver to stop or proceed, seeing to it that the bus is not overloaded, announcing stops and generally assisting passengers. Applicants are required to do a written test of Primary School standard in Irish, English and Arithmetic, including Tots.' (Totting up the fares in coin.)

Air Hostess with Aer Lingus (age 20–26). Girls only.

'Applicants are expected to have a facility of expression both verbal and written in Irish and English. Knowledge of a Continental language is a very useful additional qualification. Experience of dealing with the public is an advantage, and reception work is also useful experience.'

Qualifications to become an Air Hostess included 'an attractive appearance, a pleasing personality and capacity for hard work. The applicant needs perfect hearing, teeth and eyesight and must be between five foot two inches and five foot eight inches in height, and eight stone to nine stone seven in weight scaled to height.'

Storeboy in the Department of Posts & Telegraphs. Boys only.

'Applicants, age fourteen to fifteen years and six months, should have completed Primary School. Up to the age of eighteen storeboys are expected to attend evening Vocational Classes in Irish and two other subjects.'

Hotel Waiter/Waitress. Boys and girls.

Applicants would serve a four-year apprenticeship. During the first year of learning the trade, without lodgings, a waiter would earn a weekly wage of £4-17-6 and a waitress £5-8-0. However,

 if a male stuck with the course and showed he intended to make his livelihood as a waiter, this was reflected in the fact that during his final year as an apprentice he would earn £9-12-0 each week against just £7-17-6 for a female doing the same work.

Fashion Model. Girls only.

'Good health and a strong constitution are essential as the work makes strong demands on the stamina of the Model, who is on her feet most of the day and may frequently have to model out-of-season clothes – flimsy garments in winter conditions and heavy winter wear in summer.'

Under the heading Normal Promotion Prospects, the Department of Labour advice cautioned that a modelling career is 'necessarily indefinite and uncertain'. However: 'The experience gained by the Model in the course of her professional career can enable her to develop a number of lucrative interests if she so desires e.g. the organisation of fashion shows, fashion journalism, television wardrobe styling, publicity work, coordination in films, or she may open her own modelling agency.'

Beautician. Girls only.
Under the heading Promotion Prospects, a girl thinking of enrolling on a beauty course was advised: 'She will find promotional outlets in Instructor posts in beauty schools, executive posts in the personnel or advertising departments of cosmetic firms, and if she is a girl with journalistic talents she may become Beauty Editor of a fashion magazine.'

The Announcer in Raidió Teilifís Éireann. Boys and girls.
'Women applicants should be unmarried or widows.'

Nun. Girls only.
One of the breaks in school routine heartily welcomed by just about every boy and girl was the occasional visit from a priest, brother or nun seeking prospective recruits for their particular order, or the missions, or the religious life in general. In the mid-
1960s almost one in twenty women active in the workforce were nuns, mostly as teachers. The recruitment literature was enthusiastically dispensed in classrooms, at community events and by door-to-door Church dues collectors.

One brochure, *The Children Are Growing Up* by Richard Brenan, had this to say under the title 'Vocation To The Religious Life':

What Are The Signs That A Girl Has A Vocation To Be A Nun?

Suitability.

(a) She must be healthy enough; that is, not too weak or disabled.

(b) She must be intelligent enough: ordinary intelligence, not genius, is required.

(c) She must be a girl of good character. All that is necessary is the ordinary piety of the good Catholic girl.

That a girl may have fallen into sin, even serious sin, does not mean that she cannot make a good nun. She must with God's help turn over a new leaf and overcome any bad habits she may have got into.

As a general rule there is nothing extraordinary in the way God calls a girl to the religious life: no special interior feeling, no mysterious voice or invitation. In fact, as in most things, God makes His will known in ordinary ways.

The essential thing is a right intention, the intention of entering religion for what we call a supernatural reason, that is, some reason connected with the truths of faith, such as:

- A desire to be generous with Jesus, Who has suffered so much for us.

- A desire for the intimate companionship with Our Lord that is possible in the peace of a convent.

- A longing to pray better.
- Or to work for the salvation of the souls at home or on the mission field.
- Or to make reparation for the ingratitude or sins of others.
- Or to devote oneself to the service of Christ in the young or the old, or the sick, or the poor, or orphans, or fallen girls.

Q: What are you to do when you want to enter the convent but your parents are against it?

A: Give careful attention to their reasons. A girl should be able to answer the question: 'Can they manage without me?' If the answer is No, then she has a duty to put off or postpone entering so long as her parents are dependent on her.

A–Z

J

Jackie Lee This Dublin-born soprano sang the theme to the massively popular kids' show *White Horses*. She also supplied backing vocals for Tom Jones' 'The Green, Green Grass of Home', Engelbert Humperdinck's 'Release Me' and 'Hey Joe' by Jimi Hendrix.

John The most popular name given to newborn boys in 1963 was John, followed in by Patrick, Michael, Paul and James. Gaelicised names such as Conor, Seán, Oisín, Liam, Cian, Cillian, Darragh, Fionn, Finn and Rian, which would become popular in the twenty-first century, were almost unknown in a decade when anglophone monikers dominated.

Jules Rimet Trophy Better known simply as football's World Cup, the trophy was stolen while on view to the public in 1966 as part of a 'Sport With Stamps' exhibition in England. Following a botched attempt to extort ransom, the unknown thief dumped it and it was discovered by a collie named Pickles.

K

KAOS Where James Bond pitted his wits against the criminal organisation Spectre, the planet's most inept spy Maxwell Smart, and his partner Agent 99 pitted their halfwits against KAOS, home to an assortment of evil masterminds including Mr Big, The Claw and Siegfried.

L

Ladybird Books 'You like Peter. I like Peter. We like Peter.' From *Things We Do* and *Things We Make*, to *Puss in Boots* and *Julius Caesar and Roman Britain*, the Ladybird series was a beloved part of countless Irish childhoods.

Lugs Brannigan Ireland's most famous tough-guy cop, James Brannigan was given charge of a mobile riot squad in 1963 and he led the garda fight against the capital's gougers, juvenile delinquents and especially the so-called Teddy Boys. Parents scared manners into disobedient kids by threatening to hand them over to Lugs.

Luxy Broadcasting into Ireland from the Grand Duchy, Radio Luxembourg, which styled itself Fab 208, was one of the few places where Irish youngsters could hear the hits of the day, although the wrong weather atmospherics could distort the signal beyond recognition.

M

Mary Given a little-needed boost by the Catholic Church's first ever Marian Year in 1954, Mary was the most popular girls' name throughout the 1960s, followed by Margaret, Catherine, Ann or Anne.

Maxi Twist Served in a plastic tub, this multi-coloured swirl of ice cream mimicked the portions which had been served for some time to cinema audiences. Launched in 1968, the Maxi Twist was essentially the Mini Twist rebranded with a bigged-up name.

Me Mammy Milo O'Shea starred as Irish mammy's boy Bunjy Kennefick, who has a high-powered job in London. His interfering ultra-Catholic mother, played by Anna Manahan, does her best to foil his wooing of Miss Argyll, played by Yootha Joyce, later Mildred in the hit 1970s sitcoms *Man About The House* and *George & Mildred*. Hugh Leonard wrote this BBC sitcom.

Michael O'Hehir As a schoolboy, O'Hehir wrote to Radio Éireann seeking an audition as a sports commentator. He got the job. That was in 1938. By the 1960s he stood alone as 'the voice of Gaelic games'.

Mobile Library Throughout the decade these moveable rooms, the size and shape of freight containers, would be towed from school to school and village to village, where they'd rest for a day or two before moving on. For many communities, urban and rural, adults and children, the arrival of these mobile entertainment centres was a matter of some excitement, and orderly queues would form outside as only five or six people could file slowly along the narrow corridor inside, scanning for new additions, or eagerly anticipated returns to the shelves that lined the walls on both sides.

Top family films 1963

FLIPPER

Starring Chuck Connors, Luke Halpin, Kathleen Maguire

This hit film about the unlikely friendship between a twelve-year-old boy and a wild dolphin was produced by Hungarian Ivan Tors, who would go on to produce some of the biggest hit kids' TV of the Sixties including *Daktari* and *Gentle Ben*. Florida Keys fisherman Porter Ricks (Connors) disapproves when his son Sandy takes up with a dolphin injured by a harpoon, but the father's objections gradually fade after Flipper proves equally adept at entertaining the local kids, finding new fish stocks for the whole community, and fighting off marauding sharks. Flipper communicates with Luke in a click language remarkably similar to that used later in the decade by Skippy the Bush Kangaroo to pass on dire warnings to his human friend, Sonny Hammond.

THE GREAT ESCAPE

Starring Steve McQueen, James Garner, Richard Attenborough

Three years on from *The Magnificent Seven*, director John Sturges reunited Steve McQueen, Charles Bronson and James Coburn in an all-star cast for this Second World War POW adventure. The film features one of the most memorable chase scenes in cinema, as serial escapee Captain Virgil Hilts (McQueen) steals a motorcycle, jumps a barbed-wire border fence and leads his Nazi pursuers a merry chase before his final capture. Initial reviews were mixed. Top critic Leslie Halliwell labelled it 'overlong', *Time* said that aspects of the cinematography were 'jarring', while *The New York Times* asserted: '*The Great Escape* grinds out its tormenting story without a peek beneath the surface of any man, without a real sense of human involvement.' However, the film's stature has grown with time and it is now considered a classic.

JASON AND THE ARGONAUTS

Starring Todd Armstrong, Honor Blackman, Patrick Troughton

Presenting special-effects animator Ray Harryhausen with a lifetime-achievement award at the 1992 Academy Awards, Tom Hanks remarked: 'Some people say *Casablanca* or *Citizen Kane*. I say *Jason and The Argonauts* is the greatest film ever made.' Set in ancient Greece, the film brought to life monsters and phantoms and catastrophes with a vividness that no child could resist. While some early critics carped that it played fast and loose with the original stories and was too 'popcorn', it remains a great favourite of kids of all ages. Already a star of *The Avengers*, Honor Blackman would graduate to Bond Girl in 1964's *Goldfinger*, while Patrick Troughton would become a keystone of Saturday TV in 1966 as the second *Doctor Who*.

THE NUTTY PROFESSOR

Starring Jerry Lewis, Stella Stevens

Written and directed by its star Jerry Lewis, this send-up of *Dr Jekyll and Mr Hyde* was a huge hit and continues to turn up regularly on the afternoon TV schedules. Lewis plays nine-stone nerdy weakling Professor Julius Kelp who invents a serum that transforms him into a slick babe magnet, Buddy Love, so full of himself that love interest Stella Purdy (Stevens) can't figure out why she's so obsessively attracted to him. When Stella finally discovers that the boorish ladykiller Love and the bumbling nerd who lectures her at college are one and the same, she decides that her buck-toothed professor is the one for her. Kelp would provide the template for Professor Frink in *The Simpsons*, with Lewis doing a voice cameo as Frink's zombie father.

THE PINK PANTHER

Starring David Niven, Peter Sellers, Claudia Cardinale, Robert Wagner

The first film in what would become a long-running franchise was intended to showcase the veteran actor David Niven as the playboy jewel thief Sir Charles Lytton. However, Peter Sellers stole the show as the gormless Inspector Jacques Clouseau who is so clueless he doesn't realise that his own unfaithful wife is in league with the man he's after. One early hostile reviewer credited Sellers with saving 'a basically unoriginal and largely witless piece of farce carpentry'. *The New York Times* critic wrote: 'Seldom has any comedian seemed to work so persistently and hard at trying to be violently funny with weak material.' The public decided that Sellers' performance was worth the price of admission itself and it was a big hit.

Uncertainty, fear, anxiety and no spiritual values

Tolka Row and *The Riordans* – Ireland's Sixties soaps

Ireland's first TV soap was *Tolka Row* and, like it or not – and there was nothing for kids to like about this dour kitchen-sink drama – the children of 1960s Ireland perched in front of the set on Friday evenings with their parents and endured the shrill bickering of neighbours who weren't good friends. Telefís Éireann was fully two years old before it brought the genre to screen in 1964, largely because the national broadcaster was fearful of being accused of producing what one Christian commentator called 'an excess of drama devoted to the kitchen sink school, in which the sordid and the immoral seem to be the only things'.

The remark was made at a seminar on social communications held by the Knights of Columbanus in 1964, and the sordid and immoral prime target was *Coronation Street.* Since it first aired in 1960, *Coronation Street* had been a broadcasting phenomenon, winning a legion of Irish viewers in multi-channel land. And if *Coronation Street* was gritty by the standards of the day, the

American soap *Peyton Place* – which was inspired by the antics of the Rovers Return regulars – pushed the boundaries of taste even further while giving breakthroughs to future Hollywood stars like Mia Farrow and Ryan O'Neill.

Speaking for most of those who attended the seminar, and firing a shot across the bows of the national broadcaster, one Father Faupel insisted that Irish soaps should reflect Irish family values instead of trying to unravel the prevailing social fabric like the indecent ones beamed in from Britain. He said: 'I am sure that in this country there must be people who can present the concept of the Christian life with all its values, its virtues, its wholesomeness. I am sure you should be very conscious of the dramatic output of a Catholic country like Ireland. I was hoping that you would see a way in which you could support perhaps young script writers … especially those people who are content to see virtue in the normal.'

Another speaker, this time at a summer school themed 'The Challenge Of Television', worried aloud that the absence of a neat conclusion at the end of each thirty-minute soap episode would have a negative effect on young girls in particular. James Campbell maintained that the lack of clear-cut happy endings in ongoing soaps would produce in young viewers 'an attitude to grown-up life which is very disturbing, especially amongst girls for whom there are few positive models on television: we have fear, worry and anxiety about grown-up life. Young people need reassurance, something positive. What do they get? Uncertainty, fear, anxiety and, of course, no spiritual values.'

When it finally hit the screens, *Tolka Row* lived up to the worst fears of the Knights and their allies. In the words of the *RTV (RTÉ) Guide* after season one: 'Life in Tolka Row never runs on an even tenor. It is a battlefield of crabbed youth and age, of boy breaks with girl, of all hands on deck lads, the family ship is going on the rocks.' The Nolan family was the one most often on the rocks, as garage foreman Jack Nolan and his wife Rita attempted to smooth over the cracks between themselves and their angst-ridden Mod son, while doing their best to preserve their daughter's shaky marriage.

One of the many problems dogging *Tolka Row* was that nothing really ever happened, not that the viewer got to see, anyway. Not a week went by without some disparaging reference to Mrs Feeney's nine little 'chislers' living next door to the Nolans, but the camera never showed this rabble of rug rats. Indeed almost everything that happened in *Tolka Row* happened off camera, to be divulged only in the chitchat of the Nolans' living room. Where the Rovers Return served as a community meeting place in *Coronation Street*, Keogh's pub in *Tolka Row* never had more than one or two sour-faced customers, including the formidable local battleaxe Queenie Butler. The writing was on the wall in 1967 when the actress playing the central character of Statia left the show to be replaced with another actress attempting to slip unnoticed into the same role. Audiences couldn't accept that Statia had changed utterly overnight and now looked and sounded nothing like herself. Most of all though, *Tolka Row* was axed in 1968 because it was desperately boring. As the newspapers rolled out their obituaries for the expired soap, one writer hit the nail on the head when he pointed out that for all its attempts to explore social issues, '*Tolka Row* never stepped on anyone's toes'.

At the start of the decade the organisers of the Challenge of Television conference had petitioned the Minister for Posts &

Telegraphs to ensure that Telefís Éireann's drama output would cherish and support family values and the farming community. In a memorandum, they told the Minister that they were 'particularly concerned that the overall impact of the programmes on Irish television should not be such as to convey the image of urban or city life as the only desirable one, and that any tendency towards associating an excess of sordid themes with rural life should be avoided'.

They got their way when *The Riordans* went on air in 1965, and quickly overtook *Tolka Row* as the favourite soap of the nation's parents. As was the case with *Tolka Row*, children watched because they had no choice. In stark contrast to the static and listless Dublin-based soap, *The Riordans* took the viewer out and about *amuigh faoin spéir* into the great outdoors. In order to capture the real-life workings of a farm, the makers took the revolutionary step of bringing in the Outside Broadcast Unit, which normally covered sporting events, for exterior scenes. Prior to this, soaps in Ireland and Britain had been studio-bound affairs. As a direct result of the success of *The Riordans*, ITV launched its own rural counterpart, *Emmerdale Farm* (now *Emmerdale*), in the early 1970s.

Ten favourite children's cowboy shows

THE BIG VALLEY
Barbara Stanwyck starred as the widowed matriarch of the Barkley clan, living in the Sacramento Valley following the Civil War. The all-star cast featured future *Six Million Dollar Man* Lee Majors and *Dynasty*'s Linda Evans.

BONANZA
In the 1963 episode 'Hoss and the Leprechauns', the portly Hoss Cartwright tries to convince his family he has found a leprechaun's golden hoard. When a visiting Irish professor confirms that the little people exist, the whole town starts searching for them.

CASEY JONES
Telefís Éireann and the BBC picked up on this as perfect Saturday morning fare because it eschewed the gunfights of other shows to concentrate more on the homespun family life of train driver Casey and his Cannonball Express crew.

DANIEL BOONE
'Daniel Boone was a man, yes a big man / The rippin'ist, roarin'ist, fightin'ist man the frontier ever knew.' Having made his mark as Disney's Davy Crockett, Fess Parker kept on his coonskin cap for the identikit role of Daniel Boone.

F TROOP

The favourite TV western of them all with Irish youngsters was this zany comedy set in Fort Courage. The officer in charge was the nice-but-dim Captain Wilton Parmenter who was constantly outwitted by his black-marketeering Sergeant Morgan O'Rourke.

GUNSMOKE

The most grown-up of the small screen westerns, *Gunsmoke* enjoyed a successful pre-TV run on radio with William Conrad (later TV's fat detective Cannon) in the lead as troubleshooting Marshal Matt Dillon. The town blacksmith was played by Burt Reynolds.

THE HIGH CHAPARRAL

Big John Cannon runs the High Chaparral ranch with the help of his brother Buck and son Billy Blue. After Blue's mother is killed, Big John marries the fiery Latin beauty Victoria, but the course of true love never runs smooth, with cattle to ranch and bad guys to shoot.

THE LONE RANGER

Shot for US TV between 1949 and 1957, *The Lone Ranger* was already ancient by the time it became a regular on Telefís Éireann in the 1960s. The masked lawman and his white horse Silver were partnered by Tonto and Scout.

MAVERICK

James Garner played Bret Maverick, a motormouth card shark who travelled the Wild West and sailed the Mississippi riverboats with his brother, playing poker, getting into scrapes and usually forsaking ill-gotten gains in order to do the right thing.

THE VIRGINIAN

Loosely based on a 1902 novel of the same name and with one of the most memorable theme tunes of the decade, this series followed the adventures of the tough foreman of the Shiloh Ranch and his top hand Trampas played by Doug McClure, later parodied as *The Simpsons'* flaky Troy McClure.

Made in Taiwan – a mark of quality

There were patriotic toys, and toys kids actually wanted

Although the boys and girls were too young to appreciate it, when it came to toys, 1960s Ireland had never had it so good. One spin-off from America's baby boom of the 1950s was a huge surge in the quantity and variety of toys being designed and manufactured there, while Formosa (Taiwan) filled a gap for cheap and cheerful plastic dolls and other flimsy stocking fillers. With a range of wartime industries tapering off, factory space and production lines across the United States became available for speedy conversion to cater to the demands of the peacetime market, and millions of young families starting up in post-war America and flush with money demanded newer and better toys.

By the start of the 1960s, this boom in toymaking was beginning to make itself felt in an Ireland experiencing the first mild flushes of its own economic mini-boom. While some children perched on the knee of their local department store Santa still asked for basics like slippers or an umbrella as their Christmas wish, the popular requests now included talking dolls, electric model cars, electric toy sewing machines, and the mind-boggling range of products piggybacking on the space-race frenzy.

The modest expectations of just a decade earlier had been gleefully cast aside by a generation who wouldn't believe a word from parents who told them that in their day a bar of chocolate and an orange would have made the perfect start to their Christmas morning. In the run-up to Christmas 1962 the country's top department store, Clery's, announced the opening of the kiddies' wonderland it called Toytown. Young visitors could expect to be dazzled by: 'A wonderful display of mechanical moving models including Daisy Duck, Lion Trainer, Snake Charmer, Balloon Seller, Bell Ringer, Jack In The Box, Musical Cat, Clowns etc.' Apart from a 'large selection of dolls and prams', the top toys included three-wheeled chain-drive tricycles, Thunderbolt pedal cars, Majestic sports bikes and an 'unbreakable sleeping baby doll with washable hair'.

And there was the rub. The young children of Ireland, with not a patriotic thought between them, were completely sold on these fantastic plastic and die-cast metal playthings stamped with telltale marks of quality that any kid could instantly recognise from the TV advertisements, like Mattel and Waddington. The trouble was that in the eyes of many of their elders and betters running the country, children choosing these foreign objects of desire were guilty in some small but grave way of perpetrating treasonous anti-Irish activities.

As with TV, cinema, religion, sport and everything else, the state was certain that it knew best when it came to toys. There were tariff-protected toy factories in Dublin, Cork, Galway and Mayo, producing kids' scooters, tricycles, seesaws and wheel-barrows, while cottage workshops turned out clunky wooden 'craft' dolls, forts and puzzles. For Ireland's rulers, these craft toys were not only morally superior to imported trash, but they also supported jobs here, while keeping out imports from Communist Poland and Czechoslovakia. School principals were even enlisted by Official Ireland to badmouth foreign toys to their little charges through patriotic pep talks. But the kids didn't want worthy-but-dull home-produced playthings. One deputy, Thaddeus Lynch, came out in favour of the child's right to choose.

In the Dáil in 1960, Lynch heard out the complaints of independent TD Frank Sherwin, who said: 'I would ask the Taoiseach to do something about the junk toys and goods coming into the country from outside. Kids are being robbed. They have to pay a shilling for a small toy which is a big amount to them. If you blew on one of these alleged gelatine toys, you would dinge it. I would ask the Taoiseach to do something about all these junk toys.'

Deputy Lynch suggested witheringly that Sherwin should take up the matter of shoddy toys with Santa Claus.

What Ireland's children wanted for Christmas throughout the decade were cool things like Mattel's Chatty Cathy doll, Airfix model space rockets, and bikes with Comet wings. Of the many versions available, the most prestigious toy car of the entire decade was Corgi's 007 Aston Martin with a 'bulletproof shield' that popped up at the rear and a wicked ejector seat that guaranteed the little plastic passenger would be lost forever before teatime on Christmas Day. Girls loved pneumatic plastic Barbie, despite an *Evening Press* plea that the mothers of Ireland should try to direct their young daughters to innocent old-style rag dolls. For boys, the ultimate pressie was the new improved Scalextric, promoted as 'the most complete model motor racing system in the world'.

Each 8 December, the Catholic Feast of the Immaculate Conception, half of rural Ireland descended on Dublin for the Christmas shopping. To rustle up business during the flatlining 1950s, the owners of Clery's had hit on the inspired idea of refunding the travel fares of customers who spent over a certain amount in store, and by the start of the 1960s, for countless visitors to the capital, meeting and regrouping under Clery's clock had become a hallowed custom. For stocking fillers, decorations and assorted bric-a-brac the busiest stores in Dublin on the big shopping day of 8 December were Woolworths, Banba Toys and Hector Grey's.

A familiar sight standing outside his shop on the capital's Upper Liffey Street, attempting to entice passers-by into his Aladdin's Cave, Hector Grey was, in fact, a Scotsman called Alexander Scott. Blessed with the gift of the gab, he borrowed the Hector Grey alias from a top Australian jockey while he was working on Irish racecourses and decided to stick with it. His shelves were packed, impossibly tightly and right up to the ceilings, with such a wild array of colourful thingamajigs that young kids crossing the threshold would be stopped in their tracks, transfixed by the glory of it all.

TWENTY-FIVE TOP TOYS OF THE 1960S

007 Aston Martin

Dr No announced the presence of a new superspy in the form of Sean Connery's James Bond, and *From Russia With Love* sealed the deal, but it was with 1964's *Goldfinger* that the franchise went mega, taking more at the box office than the first two combined. As film-goers spilled out of the early screenings, however, it fast became clear that the car was the real star of this show. The boffins had assigned Bond a sleek gold Aston Martin sports car and it had all the features a top spy, or a young boy, could ever wish for. These included a bulletproof shield rising out of the boot, retractable spikes in the wheels for putting baddies off the road, concealed machine guns in the front bumper and, best of all, a passenger ejector seat. The public's reaction as the car upstaged the world's top male sex symbol prompted the film's producers to launch a must-have Corgi model in 1965 with working versions of all the film car's features. It became the best-selling model car of the year.

Action Man

Action Man arrived on these shores in the late 1960s as a lightly disguised refugee from the Vietnam War. In the early part of the decade the GI Joe action figure had been a huge hit with little boys across the United States, but after the Pentagon began its ground war in Vietnam in 1965, sales of GI Joe first slowed, then slumped, as American parents registered their disapproval. The response of Joe's manufacturer, Hasbro, was to find a European outlet for their toy soldier. In 1966 Action Man was launched in Britain and Ireland by Palitoy under licence. Action Man, 'the moveable fighting man', was, according to the thrilling TV advertisements, always 'on the lookout for action, up in mountains, down in the jungles'. Apart from the fact that Action Man was more flexible than his stiff predecessor GI Joe, the newcomer also arrived with a full wardrobe of uniforms, regalia and accessories. In other words, he was a doll that boys could dress up. This, of course, was a glaring reality that could never speak its name. The word 'doll' was banned from the Palitoy workplace, where all employees were instructed on pain of some horrible consequence to refer to the doll as an action figure.

Anything to do with space

The space race began in earnest in 1957 when the USSR first put the Sputnik satellite and then a dog, Laika, into orbit, with the USA joining in at the start of 1958. In 1962 President John F. Kennedy promised a moon landing by the decade's end, and requests to Santa for ray guns, space suits and other gadgets went stratospheric. For the older boy, the prized possession of 1969 was Airfix's model of the Lunar Module which touched down for the first moon landing that summer. Fiendishly complicated, it presented the ultimate challenge to countless young glue enthusiasts (and their fathers).

Barbie

Watching her daughter Barbie giving her dolls grown-up roles as she played, American Ruth Handler spotted a gap in the market for a doll in adult form at a time when most represented infants. She found her model in a risqué German effigy called Lilli, who was originally marketed to grown men as what one critic claimed was a 'sex toy'. Handler put the idea to her husband, who'd founded the toy-making giant Mattel, but he dismissed it as a folly. Ruth persevered, and Barbie made her debut in 1959. The kerfuffle over her pneumatic bust and sexy swimsuit propelled the doll to 350,000 sales in its first year. Reflecting on Barbie's success, the *Irish Press* lamented: 'Rag dolls, those squashy companions of our youth, have gone for good, and it seems to me that few small girls become strongly attached to their glossy descendants.

I really think that the perfection of modern dolls never can arouse the same fierce maternal instinct in children.'

Cluedo

Cluedo broke new ground as the first mass-appeal mystery game when it made its debut at the end of the 1940s. The board game brought the Edwardian trappings of an Agatha Christie stage whodunnit into the living room. The whimsical character names – Professor Plum, Mrs Peacock, Colonel Mustard – and the murder weapons, which included a candlestick, rope and lead pipe, perfectly matched the quirky setting of a rambling English country house. There was even a perfect closing line for the annual Christmas advertising campaigns: 'For adults and children only.'

Cowboy gear

The most popular TV shows during the decade included *The Virginian, Rawhide, Gunsmoke, The High Chaparral, Bonanza, The Lone Ranger, Daniel Boone* and *F Troop.* This endless stream of Westerns ensured a constant demand for cowboy and cowgirl costumes complete with hats, sheriff badges, holsters and even attachable tin spurs. Indian costumes were equally popular, while model Western forts provided small boys with their version of a doll's house.

Frisbee

'It flies. It soars. It hovers.' American husband and wife Fred and Lucile Morrison started up a small but thriving flying-disc company in California in 1938 after they were offered 25 cents for the 5-cent cake pan they were tossing to each other on Santa

Monica beach. Morrison sketched design improvements during his time as a prisoner of war during the Second World War and restarted as a manufacturer when he finally made it back to Civvy Street. The flying disc went through various incarnations before it took off for the heady heights after the Wham-O company began marketing it as a sport in 1964. By then, the disc had acquired the name by which it has become best known, taken from the Frisbie Pie Company in Connecticut. It first arrived in Ireland as The Getaway, and after the first giddy rush of excitement had passed, children the land over quickly realised that something that flies, soars and hovers with grace in sunny California can become an uncontrollable beast in the mildest Irish gale and entirely useless in the semi-permanent Irish rain.

Hula hoop

Since time immemorial children around the world had squeezed great fun out of throwing, twirling or rolling hoops made of willow, grapevine, grasses and various other materials, but it was not until 1958 that two Americans came up with the brainwave of making hoops out of plastic, copyrighting one of nature's basic shapes, the circle, and making a packet. Given a massive marketing launch by California's Wham-O toy company, the Hula hoop sparked an American craze that quickly swept the world, and by the close of 1960 global sales had passed the hundred million mark. While it remains a favourite of youngsters around the globe, the Hula hoop would never again enjoy the massive popularity it had in the 1960s.

Johnny Seven OMA

'There's no other gun like it' blared the TV adverts, and it took just one look for every small boy to believe it and want one. Over 3 feet long and weighing in at a substantial 4 lb, the Johnny Seven seemed like the real thing, only much, much better. The OMA stood for One Man Army and this multi-purpose toy weapon promised to be just that. It was a grenade launcher, an anti-armour gun, an anti-tank gun, an anti-bunker gun, a repeating rifle, a tommy gun and a fast-firing pistol. Derry band The Undertones, themselves children of the 1960s, would later pay homage to every young boy's dream Christmas present on their track 'What's With Terry?', which featured the lines: 'Then came the day Terry always did dread / Christmas had come, a present lay on his bed / A Johnny Seven or a cuddly toy?'

Lego

The Danish firm Lego (meaning 'play well') was making wooden piggy banks, cars and trucks from the 1930s, but the breakthrough came in 1947 with the end of the wartime plastic shortage. Lego launched its Automatic Binding Bricks in 1949, renaming them Lego Bricks in 1953. Along with the more finicky Meccano, Lego remained a firm favourite of Irish children throughout the 1960s, becoming big film business in the twenty-first century.

Magic-Cool electric oven set

Toy kitchen sets were commonplace in the 1960s. In addition to providing tons of fun, they gave little girls an early feel for the future of domesticity that had been ordained for most of them.

In 1967 the Magic-Cool Electric Oven migrated across the Atlantic and not only wowed the little girls of Ireland, but their brothers, mothers and fathers too. Expensive, but achievable with a bit of saving, this 79-piece set included a miniature oven, 14 baking utensils, a cookbook, 27 real cake mixes, each in their own miniature packet, and 36 birthday candles. It was an impressive package, but by far the most impressive thing about it was that it actually worked. As the adverts put it: 'The Magic-Cool Oven is fully insulated. Exterior never gets hot. Child never touches a hot pan because just a turn of a knob moves pan from oven to cooling chamber. Nichrome wire, porcelain ceramic heating element (*not* light bulb) assures even temperature. Set includes specially prepared mixes to bake 16 deliciously frosted cakes, two pies and two batches of yummy brownies.' The boys could have their 007 ejector seat Aston Martins – this was far, far better.

Meccano

The master toymaker Frank Hornby knew he had a hit on his hands when he began designing construction kits for children in 1898. Three years later in 1901 he put his miniature sets of struts, girders and rivets on the shelves, marketed as Mechanics Made Easy. He swapped this for the snappier Make & Know, which became Meccano. Given a new promotional push in the 1950s Meccano was big in the 1960s, considered by boys reaching a certain age to be a step-up from Lego. Small boys and their fathers spent many a long and frustrating evening losing tiny screws and vital parts.

Monopoly

Monopoly first appeared in 1935 and was based on The Landlord's Game devised in 1904 by Lizzie Philips. The pious Quaker woman's original intent was to explain the 'single tax' theory of economist Henry George who opposed landlordism and advocated the common ownership of land. Ironically, what started out as a lesson in sharing mutated into an exercise in 'greed is good'. Throughout the 1960s Monopoly enjoyed the same massive popularity in Ireland as across the rest of the globe, despite the fact that Irish families would have to make-do with the London edition until Ireland got its own edition in the early 1970s.

MONOPOLY

Scalextric

Scalextric became an overnight success by the evolutionary stroke of adding electricity to the moderately popular Scalex cars which ran on clockwork engines. The brand boosted its popularity with little boys (and their dads) in the mid-Sixties when it began a long association with the James Bond franchise by launching a miniature 007 Aston Martin from *Goldfinger*.

Scrabble

The game's American creator Alfred Butts calculated the precise frequency of every letter available to players by doing a painstaking letter count of hundreds of issues of *The New York Times*. Butts was no businessman, however, and his wordplay game languished neglected for a decade before American James Brunot offered to take on the project, but only on condition that Butts agree to take a royalty on every set sold instead of an upfront payment. For four years Brunot dragooned family members into making sets in a converted schoolhouse, but they were producing only 2,400 annually and losing money. The boss of the giant Macy's retail chain became a Scrabble addict while on his holidays in the 1950s, and when he discovered that his store didn't stock it, he placed a huge order. By the 1960s Scrabble was an Irish family favourite, and Butts' royalties were rolling in.

See 'n Say dolls

Mattel managed to trademark the word 'chatty' after finding huge success with their Chatty Cathy doll, which uttered eleven random bursts of silliness at the pull of a string. The company went on to introduce the See 'n Say range of talking dolls in 1965 which allowed the child to choose the precise phrase they wanted to hear by adjusting a pointer on the toy's face to a particular part of the body and pulling the 'chatty ring'. The product was so popular there were 1960s celebrity Disney versions including Winnie the Pooh and Doctor Dolittle.

Sindy

At the start of the 1960s the toy manufacturer Mattel offered the British company Pedigree a licence to produce Barbie dolls for the British and Irish markets. However, after market research showed that Barbie was a bit too risqué for the tastes of many parents on this side of the pond, Pedigree opted to go with a more girl-next-door type. Sindy arrived in 1963 bearing a remarkable resemblance to the more wholesome American doll, Tammy. Tammy's owners had also lent Sindy the slogan: 'The doll you love to dress.' Retailers were given a 45 rpm promotional disc which blared out the newcomer's CV: 'Sindy is the free, swinging girl that every little girl longs to be. Sindy has sports clothes, glamour clothes, everyday clothes – a dog, skates, a gramophone – everything … Every genuine Sindy outfit is a child's dream come true. Each one is designed for today's fashionable young women by today's leading women designers. They are authentic miniature replicas of the latest adult clothes.' Styled for the Swinging Sixties, Sindy had a great decade in Ireland.

Snakes and Ladders

This first appeared in 1943 and was based on an ancient Indian game, Ladder of Salvation, aimed at teaching kids the virtuous rewards of doing good deeds. The morality tale illustrated on the original board, and on some modern versions, is that a person can attain salvation by good actions, or suffer rebirth as a slithering beast by sinning. By the 1960s, cheapish boxed compendiums featuring several games for all the family were becoming hugely popular with Irish buyers, and the Snakes and Ladders board was inevitably at the heart of the package, often with the Ludo squares printed on the flipside.

Space Hopper

Created by an Italian company that manufactured rubber balls, the Space Hopper arrived in Ireland just in time for the first moon landing in the summer of 1969. Putting the word 'space' in the title of anything and everything was by now a jaded marketing ploy as the decade-long space race reached its climax, but kids would have loved this fun ride even if it had been called a Sit 'n' Bounce or Pon-Pon, as it was in the US and Italy respectively. Essentially a heavy orange rubber exercise ball with added ears to be clung onto as grips, and a painted-on kangaroo face, the Space Hopper was an instant hit with youngsters in Ireland and everywhere else.

Spirograph

Launched in 1965, the brainchild of designer Denys Fisher, Spirograph became an instant worldwide hit. Technically speaking, the device was a geometric drawing toy which produced roulette curves known as epitrochoids and hypo-trochoids, but that was too much information for the millions of boys and girls simply delighted to discover they could make wonderful pictures with just a pen and a few bits of plastic.

Stylophone

No sooner had the Stylophone appeared in 1968 than a debate opened up as to whether it was a toy or a proper musical instrument. Its designer, Brian Jarvis, sought a middle path when he said: 'It's like a little notebook for musicians. You stick it in your pocket and if you have an idea while you're out, you're away!' But the proper musical instrument lobby persisted, and claimed victory in the summer of 1969 when David Bowie gave the electronic device a prominent role on his breakthrough hit 'Space Oddity'. However, the commercial success of the Stylophone rested on the legions of children who bought or sought it as a novelty musical toy. At the time of its launch, it was described as 'the future of music in a box', but it could only play one note at a time and its musical range proved too limited to ever make that hype come true.

Subbuteo

In 1967 the Education Minister Donogh O'Malley lamented the fact that so many schools banned so-called 'foreign games' including association football. The Minister called for pupils to be allowed to play the games they wanted to, rather than those their teachers made them play. The soaring sales of the 'flick-to-kick' football game throughout the 1960s suggested that very few young Irish boys shared the utter distaste for 'foreign games' that older generations were trying to drum into them. Subbuteo had been around since the late 1940s, but the early kits were so basic that players had to mark out their pitch on a bed sheet provided by their mothers. However, when England were awarded the hosting of the World Cup Finals tournament for 1966, all changed utterly. As football fever gripped England in the years before and after the home nation's victory, sales rocketed. Irish children looking in from the TV sidelines were not immune. As the decade progressed, more and more accessories (managers, floodlights, etc.) arrived, but nothing ever fixed the central problem that the game itself didn't really work.

The Teddy Bear

Named for the hunting-and-shooting US President Theodore Roosevelt, the first fluffy creation was marketed as Teddy's Bear in 1903 after the creator Morris Michtom sent one to the President and got permission to use his name. Within a mere three years it was a huge hit both as a kid's toy and as a sophisticated women's fashion accessory. In 1932 Irishman Jimmy Kennedy added the familiar lyrics to the 1907 instrumental hit 'Teddy Bears' Picnic'. The Teddy Bear, in all its forms, remains a timeless toy classic.

The Train Set

Dating from the 1840s, the early toy trains were made of cast iron or wood, and often powered by steam or clockwork engines. A German firm selling doll's houses created train sets as an equivalent money-spinner pitched at boys who would continue to buy add-on features long after the initial purchase. Electric trains appeared in 1897 strictly as the playthings of the well-to-do. By the 1960s electricity had reached virtually every Irish household (though not all) and affordable mass-produced sets meant that almost every Irish household had one lurking somewhere by the end of the decade.

Operation

The inventor of Operation, American industrial design student John Spinello, was no shrewd financial operator. Having come up with the idea for the game, Spinello sold the rights to his creation to games giant Milton Bradley in 1964 for $500 and the promise of a job when he finished college. The game, which tested the player's motor skills, was a scaled-down variation on a decades-old fairground attraction. The notion of concealing the electrified hoop in a cardboard patient nicknamed Cavity Sam on an operating table was irresistible to youngsters the world over, and their parents who couldn't wait to have a go.

N

Napoleon XIV One of the novelty hits most loved and imitated by children was Napoleon XIV's psychotic single 'They're Coming To Take Me Away (Ha! Ha!)' which was about a dog driving its owner to distraction. The nearer it got to topping the US charts, the more nervous radio executives got that it might be construed as making fun of nutcases, and just as it was about to hit the summit it was banned.

Nappies Although invented in 1948, commercial disposable nappies were still a fanciful future dream in the 1960s. Washing lines groaned under the weight of sodden cloth rectangles.

Newsbeat Presented by Frank Hall, this family-friendly news roundup was the precursor to the wildly popular *Hall's Pictorial Weekly*.

-Nik Following the launch of the first space satellite, Sputnik, the Russian suffix -nik was attached to a broad variety of words through the decade, including beatnik, refusnik, peacenik and nogoodnik.

Nuclear Holocaust Along with the Child Catcher from *Chitty Chitty Bang Bang* and the monstrous, murderous Bill Sikes from *Oliver!*, the end of the world loomed large in the fears and nightmares of small children.

O

O Brother! A big favourite with Irish parents and children (if they were allowed stay up for it), this sitcom set in a monastery starred Derek Nimmo as the well-meaning but hopelessly inept Brother Dominic.

Omelettes A new way of cooking eggs coming from the continent. An Irish government representative on a diplomatic mission to Europe was famously overheard ordering an omelette for breakfast.

Waiter: 'What type of omelette would Sir like?'
Irish politician: 'An egg omelette.'

Top family films 1964

FATHER GOOSE
Starring Cary Grant, Leslie Caron

A staple of countless singalongs in Sixties Ireland, 'Pass Me By' by Cy Coleman blared over the opening credits of this all-time family favourite. It relates the unlikely love that blossoms on a South Pacific island during the Second World War between a drunken slob played by Cary Grant, and a French teacher played by Caron stranded there with seven young schoolgirls in her care. As the plot unfolds, Caron's prim character falls for the man she once thought 'a rude, foul-mouthed, drunken, filthy beast' but who turns out to be a cultured academic who dropped out of the rat race for a life of boozy contemplation. With the besotted couple seconds away from tying the knot via a radio chaplain, the pesky Japanese spoil the moment. The couple, and their love, survive the ensuing onslaught to live happily ever after.

A HARD DAY'S NIGHT
Starring The Beatles, Wilfrid Brambell

The Beatles' frantic and zany film debut documents a long day of peak Beatlemania as they travel by train from Liverpool to London for a TV show. While the Fab Four try to rest up before their big performance, Paul's eccentric granddad stirs up mischief for them. The grandfather, played by Dubliner Wilfrid Brambell (a former *Irish Times* reporter and Abbey actor), is repeatedly branded 'a very clean old man', referencing his role in the BBC's *Steptoe and Son*, where son Harold habitually called him 'you dirty old man'. Hit songs include 'She Loves You', 'Can't Buy Me Love' and 'All My Loving'. The *New Yorker* wrote: 'Though I don't pretend to understand what makes these four rather odd-looking boys so fascinating to so many, I admit that I feel a certain mindless joy stealing over me as they caper about uttering sounds.'

HEY THERE, IT'S YOGI BEAR!

Starring the voices of Daws Butler, Mel Blanc

Fond of insisting 'I'm smarter than the average bear', Yogi Bear made his small-screen debut in 1958 as a supporting character on *The Huckleberry Hound Show* and proved so popular that three years later he was given his own cartoon series. In turn, his TV show became the first cartoon to make the jump from the small screen to a full-length cinema feature with the 1964 box-office hit *Hey There, It's Yogi Bear!* Its popularity with young viewers aside, Yogi Bear was a commercial winner because the designers at Hanna-Barbera had given the characters collars. This allowed animators to keep the bodies static, redrawing only the head in each frame when they spoke, and thus reducing the number of drawings by up to 80 per cent.

MARY POPPINS

Starring Julie Andrews, Dick Van Dyke

Julie Andrews began her reign as the 1960s queen of family films picking up the Best Actress Oscar in the title role of this lavish musical melding animation and live action. The firm but kind Mary Poppins floats down from the skies on her magical umbrella to answer a job advert for a children's nurse. Sporting the worst cockney accent in film history, Dick Van Dyke hams it up as Mary's long-time fellow traveller. The nanny takes her little charges, Jane and Michael, for a walk in the park which proves to be the starting point for a mishmash of surreal scenarios, including one where some funfair horses leave their carousel to rescue an Irish fox from the pursuing hunt. The classic kids' songs include 'A Spoonful Of Sugar', 'Let's Go Fly A Kite', 'Chim Chim Cheree', 'Supercalifragilisticexpialidocious' and 'Feed the Birds', a tear-jerker guaranteed to leave not a dry young eye in the house.

MY FAIR LADY

Starring Audrey Hepburn, Rex Harrison

This Best Picture Oscar-winner was based on Dubliner George Bernard Shaw's stage hit *Pygmalion*. Arrogant linguistics Professor Henry Higgins (Harrison) wagers an academic colleague that he can transform 'guttersnipe' flower seller Eliza Doolittle (Hepburn) into an acceptable member of society with some elocution lessons and sartorial styling. In time-honoured fashion the haughty professor becomes bewitched with the beautiful student and climbs down from his sterile ivory tower. Classic songs include 'On The Street Where You Live', 'Get Me To The Church On

Time' and 'I Could Have Danced All Night,' but Hepburn's singing voice was deemed too rough to carry the performances and she was overdubbed by Marni Nixon, who had previously filled in Marilyn Monroe's high notes on 'Diamonds are a Girl's Best Friend'.

Never wallop anyone over fourteen

And never tease a fat, gangling or dull child

A 1963 edition of the popular magazine *Irish Housewife* ran a feature on 'A Day In The Life Of A Ban Garda'. The piece underlined society's fear of, and obsession with, the Juvenile Delinquent. The writer reported that in 1961, a total of 1,319 children aged thirteen and under were convicted of indictable crimes, most of them for housebreaking, shoplifting, muggings and bag-snatching. This delinquency, the reader learned, was down to: 'Lack of parental control, intemperate habits, laziness, ignorance and home conditions, and profitable crime depicted on television and cinema screens.'

Throughout the decade, crumbling old urban tenements were being demolished and the communities that had occupied them for generations were uprooted and transplanted to new estates in the suburbs. The new arrivals were often received with distrust and dismay by their new neighbours.

From *The Sunday Review*, February 1963: 'At social functions, Tuppence Ha'penny must never be asked to rub shoulders with Tuppence. In two suburban areas in County Dublin where residents associations have held dances, I have been told it was found necessary to hold two separate functions – one for the teens from the better class houses and one for the more democratic housing estates.'

In its 1966 supplement *Problems of Adolescence*, the *Children's Britannica* offered the following tips to parents on how to ward off delinquent tendencies in their offspring.

It said:

Never, never tease a fat child or a gangling child or a dull child. Take a fat child to the doctor, leave a gangling child alone and create opportunities for a dull child to succeed at something.

Don't be frightened because your daughter wants to look desirable: of course she does, that's what she's here for. Don't forbid her cosmetics – help her to use them. She can cope with the boys all right, but she needs your experience to give her style.

Give every teenager a genuinely personal box or drawer or chest for love-letters, poems, fetishes or what-have-you; and don't go near it, not even a peep.

From the age of thirteen or fourteen, give your children a clothing allowance and help them to budget. In the case of genuine disaster come to their aid.

Pay no attention to scare headlines. Their only purpose is to make you buy the paper. What keeps social problems alive in people's minds is increased social sensitivity: which is a good thing and not a cause for panic.

You're probably going to clash with your teenagers. Try to work it so that the clash is worth having. For example, it seems pointless to have a row over the length of a boy's hair, though no doubt you will tell him that you think it looks awful or you think it looks lovely. In a hundred years what is it going to matter? But you may need to kick up a real rumpus over, for example, riding a motor-bike without insurance.

Never wallop anyone over fourteen. It degrades you.

The wackiest, quackiest way of restoring the national language

Dáithí Lacha agus a chairde

The 1960 Broadcasting Act, which paved the way for the start-up of Telefís Éireann, placed the native tongue at the centre of the new service. One of the prime directives was to 'bear constantly in mind the national aims of restoring the Irish language and preserving and developing the national culture'.

The youngest viewers were targeted from early on with *Dáithí Lacha* (David Duck), billed rather optimistically as 'Telefís Éireann's wackiest, quackiest cartoon character'. According to the *RTÉ Guide* of the time: 'Dáithí himself rarely says too much (we are told that he is a shy introspective duck), but his actions speak volumes. He never moves yet never stays in the same place for very long.'

The remark that the duck in the striped underpants never moved was literally true. *Dáithí Lacha* was a cartoon in the old-fashioned print sense – the star of the five-minute show was never animated. Nor were his friends Maidhc the dog and Puisín the cat. Instead, while a single static frame filled the screen, narrator Pádraic Ó Gaora would describe the action. By the time Dáithí was retired in 1969, the thrice-weekly show had been cut back to one five-minute slot each week. Published by the Government Stationery Office as educational tools, the *Dáithí Lacha* books have become collectors' items.

To his friends he was George Boyle, but to a generation of Irish children, the nation's favourite ventriloquist was better known as Seoirse Ó Baoighill, or just plain Seoirse. Boyle popped up across the children's schedules throughout the decade, including a role in *Tír na nÓg*, but it was as the human half of *Seoirse agus Beartlai* that he found his niche playing straight man to the cheeky dummy Beartlai. Between bouts of bilingual banter, the pair introduced children's choirs, Irish dancing troupes and other cultural entertainments.

Boyle's only rival for the title of Ireland's top puppeteer was Eugene Lambert, who would hit the heights towards the end of the decade with *Wanderly Wagon*, but who cut his TV teeth on the fantasy series *Murphy agus A Chairde* (Murphy and His Friends) which was first aired in 1965. The show followed the fairy-tale adventures of Murphy, a nice-but-dim giant. Murphy's friends included Seamus, a mischievous prince, and Freddie, a fifth-rate magician. Together the friends battled an Evil Witch who was rendered powerless if separated from her magic broom. Holding the plot lines together each week was Mortimer, the Tree of Knowledge, whose fund of wisdom and learning consisted entirely of overheard gossip.

There was little gossip but lots about trees on *Amuigh Faoin Spéir*, a family favourite from its first appearance on Telefís Éireann in 1963. Produced, directed and narrated by Éamon de Buitléar, this wildlife programme combined nature studies, with the *cúpla focail* and the skilful sketches of the Dutch illustrator and naturalist Gerrit van Gelderen.

Decades later, Éamon de Buitléar recalled the show's beginnings to Jan Battles for Telefís Éireann's Golden Jubilee.

'When the series began it was completely in studio. I used to borrow animals and birds and bring them into studio. The very first programme was to be about swans. Gerrit lived on the Liffey, on Conyngham Road near the Phoenix Park, and he went out in the middle of the night and captured a swan and brought it into RTÉ. You couldn't do that nowadays, of course, because it would be quite illegal. We had the prop men build an enclosure to put the swan into.

'The show was broadcast live from the studio. I had a script and as I was talking about the animals Gerrit would stand hidden behind a large, white paper screen and draw them. For example, if I were describing a particular bird such as a swan, suddenly, as if out of nowhere, a very large letter S would begin to appear on the full TV screen as Gerrit began sketching from behind the screen. The S would quickly develop into a beautiful finished drawing of a swan. Nothing like this had ever appeared before on Irish TV. It was pure magic!'

By the late 1960s the state stepped up its efforts to resuscitate the Irish language through the power of television. The user-friendly *Buntús Cainte* guide to Irish for beginners was rolled out to adults on the telly, and integrated into the classroom with the additional aids of colourful sticky-back cut-out characters that could be moved about a blackboard sheathed with cloth. The TV programme was presented by Máire O'Neill and Aileen Geoghegan, two young women styled to appeal to Swinging Sixties youth. Transcripts of the shows – *Buntús Cainte* means Basic Speaking – were published in that week's *RTÉ Guide* 'to demonstrate how Irish learnt from *Buntús Cainte* can be used in everyday situations'. One of several counterparts to *Buntús Cainte* was *Labhar Gaeilge Linn*, billed as 'a refresher course in Irish' which ran on Radio Éireann every Monday, Wednesday and Friday. The full scripts of these 'ten-minute playlets' were reprinted in the *RTÉ Guide*. Introducing one such episode, the *Guide* announced: 'This week a hypochondriac ancient mariner visits the doctor, dentist and optician.'

A writer to the *Irish Press* appealed to parents to encourage their children to participate in the TV initiative, since 'only with the knowledge and ability to speak the Irish language can they be classified as Irishmen and women'. The correspondent went on to heap blame on the Gaelic Athletic Association for its neglectful role in bringing about the derelict state of the national language, charging that the Association was as culpable as any Irish-hating lobby group because the sports body 'has done nothing for the language'.

The manly lad will take wrongful punishment in his stride

The primary school in theory and in practice

The Functioning of the Primary School – The Theory

Throughout the 1960s the Irish National School system was run along the principles outlined by the Council of Education in a 1954 report, 'The Function of the Primary School and The Curriculum To Be Pursued in the Primary School'. A few short extracts from the report convey some idea of the environment the young child entered on their first day at school. The first purpose ordained by Official Ireland was:

THE FEAR AND LOVE OF GOD
'The school exists to assist and supplement the work of parents in the rearing of their children. Their first duty is to train their children in the fear and love of God. That duty becomes the first purpose of the Primary school.'

The Irish Language

'We do not consider that the school alone can effect the revival of Irish, but it can provide such knowledge as is necessary for its revival, encourage the use of the language and awaken a sympathetic disposition to it.'

History

According to the Council of Education, one of the chief purposes of teaching history was to instil 'manliness', together with 'toleration, charity, truth, diligence and readiness to serve'.

Physical Education/Drill

For many pupils, PE class took the form of Drill, which was closely modelled on army basic training routines. Many schools put on a Drill display for parents at Christmas or the end of the school year, which involved a mix of dance, gymnastics and military drill. According to the Council: 'Through the means of physical training the child is disciplined in the care of his health, so that he may be better fitted to fulfil God's plan.'

Regarding Accusations That The System Produces Children Lacking Basic Literacy

'Even granting, which we think to be by no means certain, that there has been some deterioration in standards, allowances must be made for the many influences which, in our day, make the work of the teacher more difficult than formerly. The cinema, the radio, the miscalled "comics", are sources of distraction which were unknown to children of earlier generations. Parental control has undoubtedly lessened and the urbanisation of our population has rendered control more difficult for many of those parents who take their duties seriously.'

THE TEACHING OF MUSIC

The Council noted a decline in 'a sympathy ... of Irish airs' amongst the young generation. It commented: 'Various causes have been suggested – the decay of the Irish language, the absence of musical training in our schools, undesirable influences from abroad, or a combination of all three ... Many of our young people have poor taste in music.'

NEEDLEWORK

Teaching young girls how to knit and sew was 'a valuable practical training for girls' in preparation for their ordained futures as home-makers. 'In larger schools where there are at least two women teachers it is obligatory (for girls aged ten to twelve), consisting throughout of knitting and hand-sewing, including darning and cutting out of garments.'

The Functioning of the Primary School – The Reality

Towards the close of 1965 a three-man investigative panel published Investment In Education, a probing review of Ireland's school system. It was damning.

Amongst its findings was that of those leaving primary school in 1962–63 (either to advance to secondary level or to quit the educational system for good) only 28 per cent had attained their Primary Certificate. The Primary Certificate indicated that the holder could read, write, add and subtract at a most basic level. Incredibly, more than half of all the eleven- to thirteen-year-olds the investigators had tried to track down

(54 per cent to be precise) had disappeared without trace from the records. In the cases of the worst schools, and there were quite a few, every single file had vanished into thin air. The report also found that almost 70 per cent of one- and two-teacher schools had no drinking water. A huge number of schools had no flushing toilets.

The findings of the report were so scathing that the *Encyclopaedia Britannica* felt it worthwhile to boil down the salient facts and present them to the concerned parents of Ireland – for two shillings and six – as part of their *Children's Britannica Advisory Guides For Parents.*

The *Children's Britannica* focused on the fact that although the state insisted that children had to attend school between the ages of six and fourteen, education was only free at primary level, which most pupils finished at the age of twelve. This created a dilemma for parents in a depressed economy. Should they encourage their children to stay on to the legal leaving age of fourteen, and perhaps stay an extra year to sit their Inter Cert, knowing that they would now have to find the funds to pay for it? Or, as many did, should they take their offspring out at the end of primary and, far from struggling to find fee money, benefit by putting them out to work? The Department of Education's dismal attempts at record keeping demonstrates there was little chance of the truant officer knocking on the door.

There was a compromise available that allowed the child stay in education until the legal leaving age, and many schools facilitated it: when willing pupils reached the point where it was time to transfer to secondary level, they just stayed put in their primary school for an extra two years, sitting in on sixth class, while their teacher topped them up with secondary-level tutoring.

This was not so much of a compromise as it might at first seem, given the Dickensian set-up of the bulk of the school system. As the *Children's Britannica* reported, 16 per cent of Ireland's national schools had just a single teacher, teaching the entire curriculum for six- to fourteen-year-olds in a single classroom. The six- to twelve-year-olds would be broken up into two groups, each tackling a three-year chunk of the curriculum, with the older hangers-on delving into the secondary curriculum. Just over half of Ireland's national schools had two teachers. Of the country's 4,864 national schools in 1963 some 1,800 had fewer than fifty pupils. A large number of Protestant schools in rural areas catered for fewer than twenty pupils. More than 2,200 teachers in the primary system had no qualification and no training for the job.

The revelations of the report, and the international embarrassment it caused, spurred newly installed Education Minister Donogh O'Malley to action. In a speech that came out of the blue in September 1966, O'Malley announced the rapid introduction of free post-primary education, the start-up of a rural school bus scheme, and a pledge to take a wrecking ball to the state's crumbling nineteenth-century school buildings.

O'Malley was true to his word, and within a couple of years many schools had moved out of their crumbling shelters into brightly lit and snug wooden prefab huts. The Minister's stated intention was that these 'temporary' prefabs would be swiftly vacated as modern schools were built at quick-fire pace. O'Malley died aged just forty-five in 1968, exactly eighteen months after he'd shocked and dismayed his Fianna Fáil party with his ambitious and costly statement of intent for Irish education. Half a century after they went up, many of his 'temporary' prefabs are still busy places of learning.

A major concern highlighted in the 1965 report was that Irish schoolgirls were virtually barred from taking any science subject, while modern languages were effectively off limits to many boys. To combat this segregation, Telefís Scoile was launched in April 1964 to present tuition from TV experts who, in many cases, were expected to have a better grasp of their specialist subjects than their counterparts in the classroom. Telefís Scoile was an immediate success, and within three years 90 per cent of the – still few – schools teaching science had availed of the government grant to buy a television set for the purpose of tuning in.

But the TV set in the classroom was misleading if taken as a sign that a modern, liberal, progressive spirit had suddenly percolated into the Irish school system. Right to the end of the decade the prevailing national school regime was harsh, and that in secondary generally harsher. The schoolboys and schoolgirls were subjected to a regimen worthy of the Irish Army. There was a lot of militaristic parading and a lot of militaristic drill. Commands were issued in Irish, and often barked in a severe tone. The most common included '*Dul a chodladh*' (go to sleep), '*Oscail an fuinneoig*' (open the window) and '*Ciúnas!*' (silence!).

Corporal punishment was an everyday and unavoidable fact of 1960s school life. Under the prevailing legislation teachers, who acted *in loco parentis*, were entitled to administer the same 'reasonable and moderate chastisement' as a responsible parent, but no more than that. Taking a wide interpretation of this, educators employed the leather strap, the rattan cane, the birch and other means to instil fear, obedience and learning. Almost every teacher, male and female, lay and clerical, either carried one of these assault weapons with them or knew where to get one at short notice. Supporters of corporal punishment argued that once the short, sharp shock had been administered, the errant pupil could be returned immediately to the classroom, while suspensions from class or from school meant lessons missed.

As the 1960s opened, the Dickensian harshness of the general school regime had softened very little over many decades, despite mounting public pressure for a less penal approach. As early as 1946, in response to softening public opinion, and a greater willingness of parents to intervene, new Department of Education rules restricted corporal punishment to 'grave transgressions'. There were other rule changes intended to rein in the worst excesses of sadistic teachers. Mere failure at lessons should not now merit a beating, and any beatings handed out must be administered by, or authorised by, the school principal. Only 'a light cane or rod' was permitted, and only the open hand of the victim could be struck, as opposed to the dreaded, excruciating rap on the knuckles. The boxing of ears and pulling of hair by teachers was specifically forbidden.

But as the 1960s bore down fast, these rule changes appeared more and more a meaningless paper sop to concerned parents, while the government showed no real interest in challenging the way schools ran themselves. Senator Owen Sheehy Skeffington told the Seanad that the restrictions were being flouted to 'brutalising effect' on the nation's children. He proposed a ban on the caning of little girls between the ages of four and fourteen, as a halfway house to an end to the beating of small boys.

The Senator explained: 'My reason for proposing it be abolished in the case of girls is that it seems to me that such a motion is likely to be more widely accepted, not only in this House but outside, than if I were to propose the abolition for both boys and girls, because, in the case of girls, there can be no valid argument about 'gangsters' and 'little toughs' and 'little hooligans', as sometimes is argued in relation to the beating of small boys, even small boys of eight.'

Skeffington's appeal fell on deaf ears. Shortly afterwards, Dr Noel Browne raised the subject of a recent court case where a headmaster was found guilty in court of assaulting a pupil. Education Minister Jack Lynch confirmed the man was still at his post with the Department's blessing. Asked if the Minister considered the guilty party 'a fit person' to run a school, Lynch replied: 'I do.'

Time and again throughout the 1960s, government politicians stood up in the Dáil and Seanad and argued bluntly that it would take money the State did not have to ensure greater child protection in the general school system, and the notorious industrial schools and borstals. The government was not willing to pay, and that was that. In 1963, when Meath County Council petitioned Health Minister Sean MacEntee to allow it to increase its annual grant to the Irish Society for the Protection of Children from £20 to £50, they were told they could have an extra £5 for the year.

MacEntee told the Meath Councillors that the prevention of child cruelty 'is concerned more with social than with health matters and does not, therefore, merit a grant from health funds of the order proposed by the Health Authority. The Society is essentially one which, by the nature of its work, should in my view seek to be supported by public subscription rather than by subvention from the funds of the local or central authorities'.

From the first day of the 1960s to the last, it was an everyday fact of school life that even the youngest pupils could be plucked from their desk and made to stand facing a corner or at the back of the classroom until the end of the lesson, awaiting six of the best. The long list of offences ranged from disruptive behaviour, to arriving late, to getting a question wrong.

Perhaps most unfairly treated of all were left-handed children, known in the Irish as *citógs*. Variously translated as 'rogue', 'strange' or plain 'stupid', these unfortunates were the victims of a widespread campaign by teachers to 'correct' their sinister defect by forcing them to use their right hand for writing and every other function. Deeply damaging to young minds, this medieval practice clung on in some schools and with some individual teachers well into the 1960s.

Children who felt aggrieved by the Irish school system of hard knocks were told by Church and state, by a great many parents, and most of all by the school authorities themselves, that nobody likes a telltale.

The following is a short extract from the children's advice pamphlet *The Boy's Own* by Reverend T. A. Finnegan.

HARD TIMES AT SCHOOL

Never let anything 'get you down'. You may have a tough time in school from one or two or more of the teachers. But then, you may deserve it ... Our human nature is very lazy, and like the lazy horse we often need that painful sting of the stick to get us moving.

It is possible of course that a boy may be blamed or punished in the wrong. He may not be believed when he is telling the truth. A teacher may be 'down' on him for no apparent reason.

It is here, above all, that courage is needed. Most of us can face up to the blame when it is deserved. But it takes a strong man to rise above blame when it is undeserved, and not make him spiteful or bitter. A boy who is small-minded, wrapped up in his own importance, if he happens to be wrongly blamed or punished once or twice, will go around denouncing not only the teacher in question, but all the teachers in the school and even the school itself. The manly lad, on the other hand, will take these little crosses in his stride.

Turn your losses into gold by offering them up to Our Lord in return for what He has suffered for you. You have a long way to go before you are treated as badly or unjustly as He was.

Choirs, ceilís and clerics – Christmas Day on Telefís Éireann

Priests, prayers, carols and not much for the kids

On that first Christmas Day of the 1960s, Radio Éireann opened at 10.25 a.m. with the weather forecast. This was followed by High Mass, seasonal music, Church of Ireland Morning Prayer, Carols from the Continent and Music For Hospitals, before a five-minute break for the News at 1.30. From lunchtime until closedown at midnight it was carols, ceilís, and song and dance almost all the way, with just two shows tailored for children. One was *The School Around The Corner*, with host Paddy Crosbie as the friendly headmaster, and the other was a Junior Red Cross party from a Dublin convent school.

Along the border counties and the east coast, the few thousand homes with televisions had a choice from the kids' menus served up by the two British stations. The BBC's highlights included an episode of the western *Wells Fargo*, *Billy Smart's Circus*, *What's My Line*, *Tonight With Harry Belafonte* and, smack bang in the middle of the day, *Walt Disney; The Story of a Man Who Has Become a Legend*. The homage to

Disney would have had the automatic vote of almost everyone looking in from the Republic, as Ulster Television's rival across the schedule was *Home For Awhile*, in which: 'Jo Douglas talks to members of the Forces overseas and brings their record requests to the families at home.' Not that Radio Éireann was remiss in celebrating our own troops serving abroad, in this case away on a UN peacekeeping mission. A programme entitled *The Day In The Congo* was billed as: 'Ireland and Africa join in celebrating Christmas.'

By the Christmas of 1965, five short years later, the television set had become a fully integrated part of the Christmas Day ritual in countless Irish homes. Loaded with civic responsibility and a deep deference to the Catholic Church, Telefís Éireann typically served up a Christmas schedule that put edification above entertainment.

So Christmas Day opened at 10 a.m. with Mass, followed by Pope Paul's *Urbi Et Orbi* address, followed by non-stop religious fare until lunch when some welcome froth finally arrived via Andy Williams, *Lassie* and a children's hospital visit by *School Around The Corner* host Paddy Crosbie. Senior churchmen continued to frequent the home channel until closedown.

The top-rated Telefís Éireann shows for Christmas week 1965 were, in order, *The Late Late Show*, *Tolka Row* (Dublin city soap), *School Around The Corner*, *Quicksilver* (quiz), *The Virginian*, *Club Ceili*, *The Way of All Flesh* (ancient slushy film), *Life of O'Reilly* (music), *The Fugitive*, *The Riordans* and *Teen Talk*.

With the advent of BBC2 the previous year, Irish viewers in multi-channel land now had four stations to choose from. By the time Telefís Éireann had reached its first non-religious show of the big day, UTV had already served up *Stingray*,

Fireball XL5, *Robin Hood* and *Rudolph The Red-nosed Reindeer*, with panto, *The Beverly Hillbillies*, *Thunderbirds*, *The Big Valley* and Bruce Forsyth piling in behind with a sackful of kiddies' treats.

While a tad more staid, the BBC was still a big lure from Telefís Éireann for those who could get it, starting with a breakfast serving of *Laurel & Hardy* and onward with *Billy Smart's Circus*, *Dr Who*, *Ken Dodd*, *Val Doonican*, *The Black & White Minstrels* and *Christmas Top Of The Pops*.

At the close of Christmas week 1965, Telefís Éireann stayed on air extra late so that the last programme of 1965 and the first of 1966 would be a stirring recitation of the 1916 Proclamation, as the nation geared up for a year-long orgy of Easter Rising commemorations.

Most Watched Telefís Éireann TV Shows
Christmas Week 1967

1 *The Riordans*

2 *The Late Late Show*

= 3 *Tolka Row*

= 3 *Sing North, Sing South*

5 *Winchester '73* (film starring James Stewart)

= 6 *The Good Old Days*

= 6 *Calamity Jane* (film starring Doris Day)

= 8 *The Forsyte Saga*

= 8 *The Avengers*

= 8 *The Invaders*

A–Z

P

Political Correctness A concept that had no place in 1960s Ireland. An *RTÉ Guide* plug for the matinee film *Geronimo* was typical of its time: 'One of the most savage bands of North American Indians were the Apaches, whose spasmodic and unpredictable attacks on the early Californian settlers prevented them for years from establishing a settlement.'

Post Office Savings Stamps Sixties kids were encouraged to invest part of their pocket money in sixpenny Post Office saving stamps which were stuck into special savings books. The scheme was such a hit with youngsters that the Post Office extended it to adults. Issuing stamps valued at two shillings, it advertised them as A New Kind Of Grown Up Savings Stamp.

Q

Queenie Butler The scheming busybody Queenie Butler was forever trying to sabotage the best-laid plans of the long-suffering Nolan family and their hard-pressed neighbours on Ireland's first soap, *Tolka Row*.

R

Rollers Or hair curlers. Strange spiky rubber tubes generally found on the dressing tables of mothers.

S

Smiths Crisps In 1963 Smiths relaunched in Ireland with its 'new' crisps priced 3d and an advertising campaign featuring an image of the Irish threepenny bit illustrated with a hare. Through the rest of the decade Smiths would challenge Tayto's market dominance by running hugely popular 'collect ten packets'-style offers based on *Thunderbirds*, *The Man From UNCLE* and other hit children's TV shows.

Sport and You Friday night youth TV show presented by Brendan O'Reilly. The spindly-legged ex-high-jump champion also presented the Saturday evening sports results. Much to the annoyance of the broadcast crew, he would habitually sprint into the studio seconds before the weekly live broadcast and plonk himself behind the desk. On one occasion, the crew covertly removed his presenter's chair. O'Reilly arrived, as usual, just in the nick of time. There was no chair and he was 3–2–1, on air. He had to present the programme squatting in mounting discomfort behind the desk pretending to be seated.

Top family films 1965

CLARENCE, THE CROSS-EYED LION
Starring Marshall Thompson, Cheryl Miller

After hitting box-office gold with *Flipper* in 1963, producer Ivan Tors returned with a brace of animal-themed efforts in 1965, *Zebra In The Kitchen* and *Clarence, The Cross-Eyed Lion*. While the public gave his zebra a wide berth, they found the notion of a friendly cross-eyed lion irresistible, and the film was quickly transferred to the small screen as *Daktari*, which kept on Marshall Thompson as the dreamy veterinarian Dr Marsh Tracy, and Cheryl Miller as his daughter Paula, a determined campaigner for animal rights. The lead characters were based on the real-life Dr Antonie Harthroon who ran an animal orphanage in Kenya, and invented the M99 sedative drug and developed the Capture Gun, which shot knockout darts to allow animals be rescued without injury. Clarence had a stunt double, Leo, who had his own lion make-up artist to allow him look like Clarence in close-up shots.

DOCTOR WHO AND THE DALEKS
Starring Peter Cushing, Roy Castle, Jennie Linden

While *Doctor Who* continued to run weekly in black and white on BBC TV, its big-screen spin-off was given the full widescreen Technicolor treatment. In a plot line reminiscent of *The Time Machine*, the Doctor and his young pals arrive on a planet where two distinct species have evolved, the peaceful Thals and the belligerent mutant Daleks. After a series of close calls, the earthlings manage to prevent a nuclear holocaust and defeat the Daleks. The Daleks were originally supposed to be armed with flame-throwers, but these were downgraded to gas-spurters on fire-safety grounds. The Daleks were an instant international hit, with several dispatched to the Cannes Film Festival while others were the stars of Belfast's 1965 Christmas festivities when they 'invaded' Ann Street where the Lord Mayor was waiting to greet them.

THE GREAT RACE

Starring Jack Lemmon, Tony Curtis, Natalie Wood, Peter Falk

Co-written and directed by Blake Edwards, fresh from striking box-office gold with the Inspector Clouseau films, this slapstick-on-the-hoof affair was the most expensive comedy ever made up to that time. A precursor to Hanna-Barbera's cartoon series *Wacky Races*, the plot line revolved around the rivalry between the dastardly Professor Fate (Lemmon) and the clean-cut hero The Great Leslie played with cartoonish gusto by Tony Curtis. The pair compete to win a motor race from New York to Paris, and also for the love of the strong-willed photojournalist Maggie Du Bois (Wood). The white-clad good guy allows his evil nemesis to win the race, but his real prize is to get the girl. The film ends with Leslie and Maggie tying the knot, and the Eiffel Tower getting accidentally blown up.

THAT DARN CAT

Starring Hayley Mills, Dean Jones, Dorothy Provine, Roddy McDowell

Darn Cat, aka 'DC', is a sleuthing Siamese tomcat who happens upon a burglary where an elderly woman is being held hostage by a brace of villains. Darn Cat inevitably becomes involved in the drama, and soon becomes the focus of a police surveillance operation. A number of romances between the human characters add to the plot intrigue before it emerges at the end that Darn Cat has been doing some romancing of his own, closing the film by taking his new sweetheart and their kittens on a family prowl. With tongue in cheek *The New York Times* gushed approvingly: 'The feline that plays the informant, as the FBI puts it, is superb. Clark Gable at the peak of his performing never played a tomcat more winningly. This elegant, blue-eyed creature is a paragon of suavity and grace. It's an entertaining picture.'

THOSE MAGNIFICENT MEN IN THEIR FLYING MACHINES

Starring Stuart Whitman, Sarah Miles, Terry Thomas, Robert Morley

In 1909, a mere six years after the Wright brothers made the first manned flight of 37 metres, Frenchman Louis Bleriot astounded the world by piloting his flimsy aircraft across the English Channel to claim a £1,000 prize offered by the *Daily Mail* newspaper. Loosely based on that race, this knockabout comedy featuring Benny Hill, Eric Sykes and Tony Hancock amongst a cast of thousands of familiar faces was a huge international box-office hit. It was admired by the critics too, with *Variety* calling it: 'As fanciful and nostalgic a piece of clever picture-making as has hit the screen in recent years.'

The latest powder, hair-sheen, skin-smoother, bust-developer, bust-reducer, foundation garment

Advice to parents on dealing openly and frankly with You-Know-What

*E*ncyclopaedia Britannica* marketed itself heavily in Ireland in a period when the door-to-door encyclopaedia sales-man was still a common feature of the suburban landscape. The *Children's Britannica* offshoot targeted parents with young families.

The following tips are extracted from the *Children's Britannica* 1963 supplement entitled *Parents' Guidance For Children's Sex Education.*

SEX EDUCATION – WHAT PARENTS CAN DO

In every case of extra-marital pregnancy the parents must surely be to blame because they have failed to give their girl a sound understanding of the real nature of sex. Boys can have troubles too. They may be solicited by homosexuals at school, in public lavatories, or almost anywhere. Modern opinion has swung away from regarding homosexuals as criminal, and recognises that in very many cases homosexuality is as much a sickness as is measles, and needs proper treatment. Yet to realise this does not reduce the harm that can be done to a boy if he is lured into homosexual practices, and by far the best protection is for him to be so well informed about sexuality and puberty and the biological side of his own nature that the whole matter of sex is far too interesting and too astonishingly ingenious for him to be perverted in this way or any other.

When To Begin

The first question about sex or birth or reproduction is perhaps the most vital moment in the relationship between a child and his parents, for it is at this moment that his trust in them can be easily shattered, not just for the time being but permanently.

The child wants a simple answer to a simple question and not a long and perhaps boring lecture on the comparative physiology of pre-natal nutrition in various orders of mammals, or on bridal customs among the more obscure tribes of New Guinea.

Obviously it would be a mistake to dwell continually upon the morbid or the unusual – upon homosexuals, Siamese Twins, and Caesarean operations.

Ways To Help An Adolescent

 Make children aware of the heavy sales pressure which will surround them as they grow up. Pictures of nudes and near-nudes, busts and slinky shapes or elegant feminine legs may be used to advertise almost anything a youth might buy. Curiously enough, girls

are also attacked through female glamour – always with the idea in the background that they must catch up with the latest powder, hair-sheen, skin-smoother, bust-developer, bust-reducer or foundation garment if they are going to beat their competitors in the race to get a boyfriend.

A girl can become so bound up in her own appearance that she is made self-centred and her character fails to develop. Boys can be led to regard girls not as companions and individuals but as assembly kits of busts and stockings and nylons.

Hippie schools – not in our back yards

Most Irish children's idea of a hippie was Goldie Hawn

By the late Sixties, one of the greatest fears harboured by right-thinking Irish parents was that one or more of their offspring would fall under the evil spell of weird rockers, eastern mysticism and suspect gurus, and wind up a hopeless dropout. Young children and teens, on the other hand, were instinctively drawn to the colourful clothes and playful patois of the Flower Power generation. Here was something different and fun, and a radical change from the early part of the decade when all boys wore the crew-cut hairstyle of astronauts, and girls were dressed like miniature versions of Mary Tyler Moore or Jackie Kennedy. Cementing the notion in young Irish minds that hippies were great craic was the big Sunday night TV comedy fest *Rowan & Martin's Laugh-In*, which featured the body-painted Goldie Hawn and her pals as a band of deeply dippy far-out figures of fun.

So when a north Dublin fishing village was invaded in 1969 by a band of hippies with plans to set up an alternative school system, the local youngsters thronged in large numbers to gawk at a freak show that quickly went global.

'Hippies Take Option On Island', trumpeted the *Daytona Beach Morning Journal*. The Florida paper reported breathlessly that a large landing party of longhairs had fetched up in Skerries just days after London police evicted them from their Piccadilly squats. Led by the self-styled King of the Hippies, Sid Rawle, the refugees said they had put down a $4,800 deposit on uninhabited St Patrick's Island off the coast. Their plan was to establish a commune, which, according to the Daytona paper, would 'start with 500 British drop-outs'.

The *Montreal Gazette* wrote that Rawle and his sponsors, including a jet-setting swami and the beat poet Allen Ginsberg, would have 'no difficulty' raising the full $48,000 asking price. Even more disturbingly, one spokesman said: 'We will offer facilities for the IRA if they want them.' Local resident Sean Rooney told the Canadian paper: 'I don't like the idea. Imagine having that big bunch of unwashed wastrels out there.'

The more the hippies clarified their plans for St Patrick's, the more the plain people of Skerries vented their outrage. The would-be settlers saw St Patrick's as the first of many alternative island communities around the British Isles, housing some 20,000 dropouts (except they objected to the term 'dropouts', preferring 'heads'). They would build their own schools which would not 'process' young minds, but encourage free-thinking and free expression. Thugs would be barred, but not drugs.

Striking while the iron was hot, the hippies hired a boatman for a trip to the island 2 miles offshore. Another Florida newspaper, *The Sarasota Journal*, opened its report: 'Swami Vishnu Devananda stood on his head with joy. His two hippie companions cried: "This is wild! This is beautiful" Irish tempers boiled.'

Head-standing photo opportunities were a favourite party trick of the millionaire swami, while the paper described Rawle as 'clad in white pajamas and an Arab cloak'. The natives, it noted, were not amused, pledging to 'fight to keep the island from being desecrated'. Local councillor and future government minister Ray Burke thundered: 'They will be stopped!' Reporting that St Patrick's was currently home only to a huge colony of vicious monster rodents, *The Sarasota Journal* headlined the story 'Irish Isle Folk Prefer Rats To Hippies'.

 The prospect of Skerries becoming a world capital of wanton sex, drugs and rock 'n' roll concentrated minds, and in the space of days a range of alternative uses for the island were put forward. Some proposed that it could be turned into a botanical garden for tourists, while rumours circulated that Dublin businessmen had applied for two pub licences for the island.

A town meeting was called under the aegis of the Skerries Development Council. Press reports described 'a carnival atmosphere' at the gathering, which didn't go quite to plan for the objectors.

According to one report: 'Objections to the hippie isle plan were voiced and many people, mainly middle-aged, told the hippies in plain language that they were not wanted in Skerries, but when it came to a show of hands the residents were split. Some people had decided they had no objections.' In fact, according to another report: 'The hippies' representative, Mr Frank Harris, a poet, won several ovations when answering questions from the floor.'

Harris told the crowd: 'We are not bringing in thousands of screaming, long-haired, drug-ridden, sex-starved hippies. We want to use the island as a living laboratory, to find a way of life. If there is no water on the island, then our project falls through.'

There was no fresh water on the island, and the giant rats proved even more fearsome than the hippies had originally thought, when they discovered that a couple of years earlier the authorities had released almost forty large Manx cats, expecting them to make short work of the rats. When the officials came back some months later, they found that the rats had killed and eaten all the cats. There were other reasons the project fell through. The political establishment was already trawling the planning and property laws to make sure the hippies never cemented one brick on top of another on St Patrick's.

But no sooner had one door shut than another opened, and when word reached The Beatles' Apple HQ of the hippies' defeat in Skerries, John Lennon summoned Sid Rawle and offered him the Mayo island of Dornish in Clew Bay which he'd bought two years earlier during the recording of the *Sergeant Pepper* album.

A child of Sixties Westport, the town facing out on Clew Bay, Maureen McKee had entered her teens by the time John Lennon invited the homeless hippies to set up camp on Dornish. She recalls: 'The media would have painted us as completely remote and Clew Bay almost as if nobody was living there, but there were people living on a number of islands at the time. People would have been used to sailors and traders. There was a lot of trade went through Westport.'

Maureen and her young friends were 'huge fans' of The Beatles and immersed in the pop music of the day. She says: 'We tuned into Radio Luxembourg. And *Spotlight* was our magazine. We had hops which the teens would go to. The hops weren't showbands, they were all records. When you were past your early teens you were allowed to go to their more grown-up nights. You'd have the like of the Gallowglass Ceili Band, Margo, and The Miami with Dickie Rock. You'd have a marquee in the summer and it might stay for two weeks in Linane and two weeks in Clifden. And you had all the big showbands every night for the two weeks. It was a big topic with the teenagers at the time that John Lennon had bought an island here. We were excited about it. We weren't going to be caught up in drugs and all that.'

By the time the hippies invaded Skerries in 1969, John Lennon had owned the 19 acres of Dornish for two years. Lennon's original intention was to build a getaway for himself, wife Cynthia and infant son Julian. Shortly after buying Dornish the Beatle arrived to inspect his pet project. The solicitor who had handled the purchase, Michael Browne, told this author: 'I arranged to bring him out on a charter boat supplied by boatbuilder Paddy Quinn. It was a strict condition there was to be no disclosure of the owner.'

On that first scouting trip John did his best to be Mr Ordinary. Browne recalled: 'He was very pleasant and very practical. He was very interested in costings and he was determined to build a house that fitted in with the local architecture. All of his entourage were business types in suits except for one hippy in a kaftan called Magic Alex. But even he was there on business. I asked what he was there for and John explained that he (Alex) was working on a mechanism to stop people copying Beatles records. John was very businesslike. There was nothing airy-fairy about him. He wanted somewhere to provide him with isolation, but that would also be close to his work bases in Liverpool and London.'

John's marriage to Cynthia began to crumble and his plans for a family holiday home were long-fingered. In May 1968 she arrived back early from a trip to find John shacked up with Yoko Ono. Precisely thirty-one days later John and Yoko were in Clew Bay as an official item. He'd had a caravan, painted in psychedelic swirls, floated over from the mainland on a jerry-built raft. However, when he and Yoko arrived by helicopter shortly afterwards they thought the better of roughing it and lodged at the luxury Great Southern Hotel in the village of Mulranny.

The whirlwind of events that followed included their famous bed-in, their marriage and the toxic break-up of The Beatles. Dornish became an afterthought until John got wind of the serial squatter Sid Rawle on the lookout for somewhere to plant a new age commune.

Born to a gypsy mother and a farmer dad who was thrown off his holding, the semi-literate Rawle wanted all land to be confiscated from its owners and redistributed equally amongst the people. He was a fanatical campaigner for equality, but saw himself as first amongst equals, styling himself King of the Hippies. To emphasise the point, he dressed in the flowing robes of a high priest. Rawle assembled some thirty English dropouts and they made their home on Dornish in two large Army surplus tents. The commune became so well known that post would arrive addressed simply to Hippie Island, Ireland. 'It was heaven and it was hell,' Rawle later recalled. It was mostly hell.

The island was lashed by storms which blew the tents inside out. Crops failed. Their trips to the mainland to buy supplies with their meagre finances were met with suspicion by some and outright hostility by a small few who organised into an anti-hippie committee.

The hippie invasion of Dornish went the same way as the hippie invasion of Skerries.

Ten top TV children's sci-fi shows

STAR TREK

Captain Kirk, Mister Spock and the crew of the USS *Enterprise* boldly go where no show had gone before, in a series part inspired by Jonathan Swift's *Gulliver's Travels*.

STAR TREK

DOCTOR WHO

The regenerating Time Lord and his young female assistants explore time and space in a police phone box bigger inside than out. Even though they couldn't climb stairs at the time, the Daleks were the real stars of the early days.

THE TIME TUNNEL

Two scientists are cast adrift in a swirling vortex of past and future ages during experiments on the Time Tunnel. Tony and Doug tumble helplessly along the infinite corridors of time, always managing to bump into some giant of history like Caesar or Hitler.

LAND OF THE GIANTS

The three crew members and four passengers of the suborbital spacecraft *Spindrift* are sucked into a space warp that crashes them onto a planet where everything is twelve times (not eleven, not thirteen) normal size. The same giant matchbox features week after week.

STINGRAY

'Stand by for Action! We're about to launch *Stingray*! Anything can happen within the next half hour!' Set in the year 2064, *Stingray* charts the adventures of the World Aquanaut Security Patrol (WASP) who police the world's oceans.

THE INVADERS

The Invaders: alien beings from a dying planet. Their destination: the Earth. Their purpose: to make it 'their' world. David Vincent knows that the Invaders are here, that they have taken human form. Somehow he must convince a disbelieving world.

LOST IN SPACE

It's 1997 and the Space Family Robinson set out to found a new colony millions of light years from Earth. Sabotaged by the whinging Dr Smith they planet-hop around the galaxy encountering exotic creatures including an oversized talking carrot.

VOYAGE TO THE BOTTOM OF THE SEA

Admiral Nelson and Captain Crane voyage the seven seas in the world's first nuclear submarine, the *Seaview*, in a spin-off from the film of the same name, while recycling the ambitious props from said blockbuster.

THE CHAMPIONS

Craig Sterling, Sharron Macready and Richard Barrett are endowed with the qualities and skills of superhumans – gifts given to them by an unknown race of people when their aircraft crashes in the backyard of a lost Tibetan civilisation.

THE OUTER LIMITS

There is nothing wrong with your television set. Do not attempt to adjust the picture. We are controlling transmission. We will control the horizontal. We will control the vertical. You are about to experience the awe and mystery which reaches from the inner mind to … The Outer Limits.

Stop The Lights! Top TV quiz shows

One flop was the unfortunately titled *What's Wrong*

The first quiz show on Telefís Éireann was *Jackpot*, a test of general knowledge for all the family. Presented initially by Gay Byrne and followed by Terry Wogan, *Jackpot* ran from the opening week of the new service until the 1965 summer break when the national broadcaster cut back hours so that everyone, including their staff, could take advantage of the good weather.

Telefís Éireann's *Jackpot* bore a striking resemblance to ITV's popular *Criss Cross Quiz* which combined the game of noughts and crosses with question-answering skills. The ITV show spawned *Junior Criss Cross Quiz* specially tailored for children. One of its 1960s presenters was the Northern Ireland football captain Danny Blanchflower, who led Tottenham Hotspur to the English League and Cup double in 1961.

Jackpot was replaced in 1965 with *Quicksilver* hosted by the genial Bunny Carr, not always ably assisted on the keyboards by Norman Metcalfe whose role was to provide musical hints to the answers. The eccentricity of Norman's contributions became part of the show's appeal, as viewers attempted to work out the link, if any, between the clue and the required answer. On one occasion the pianist played the tune of 'Meet Me In St Louis' to indicate that the correct answer was 'Meath'.

The show travelled the country and the contestants were chosen from the studio audience by tickets drawn from a drum. Men were assigned blue tickets and women pink. The prize money started at three pence, which was paltry even for the day. There were thirty lights on the board and the quicker a contestant answered the question that more lights remained lit for the next question. If they were playing for sixpence and there were ten lights still lit up, the player won ten sixpences, or six shillings. A contestant could pass on a tricky question by shouting 'Stop the lights!' and the catchphrase entered the lexicon of Irish life. 'Stop the lights' remains popular shorthand for feigned wonderment.

While *Quicksilver* hovered around the top of the ratings throughout the decade and extended its long and prosperous run into the 1980s, other home-produced quiz shows failed to catch on. One flop was the unfortunately titled *What's Wrong*, which required contestants to identify errors in various pictorial presentations. Another short-termer was the charades show *Take My Word* which featured Al (brother of Gay) Byrne coaxing mimes out of stars of the Irish stage and screen.

Hosted by question master Chris Curran, the popular *Mark Time* had a ticking stopwatch as its gimmick, and pitted together two teams drawn from boys' and girls' secondary schools nationwide. *Mark Time* fared better than the station's forlorn attempt to shoehorn an Irish-language quiz right into the heart of the frothy Saturday night schedule in 1967, immediately after *The Monkees* and *The Avengers*, and before *The*

Virginian. Presented by the successful tenor and future circuit court judge Liam Devally, *Ceist Agam Ort* (I Have A Question For You) arrived in 1968 and departed soon after. Devally would eventually return to the format as the second host of the popular *Cross Country Quiz* which went on air towards the close of the decade.

Originally presented by Peter Murphy, *Cross Country Quiz* tested the general knowledge of the country's farmers, as represented by teams from branches of Macra na Feirme. As an in-demand radio broadcaster hailed as 'the voice of rural Ireland' and as the National Organiser of Macra na Feirme, Murphy was doubly qualified for the role. *Cross Country Quiz* became an instant ratings-grabber, and the inter-county rivalry could inspire great passion. One production of the show at Tipperary town hall 'broke up in confused uproar', according to the *Irish Independent,* after the quizmaster declared Wexford the winners by four points while outraged Clare supporters in the audience protested that their team had won by two points. Scuffles in the hall were accompanied by cries of 'Bunglers!' and 'Shame!'

Family quiz shows like *Quicksilver* produced a regular trickle of complaints to the RTÉ authority and the newspapers that the questions were too dumbed down. From a distance of decades, a more valid criticism is that the general knowledge required was anything but general, reflecting a far narrower and more insular world view that was prevalent in Ireland at the time.

For much of the decade, the *RTÉ Guide* ran the *Do You Know Quiz,* a weekly general test for all the family. Here's one from January 1965.

Q1: In which Irish town is there a street called The Island Of Geese?

Q2: Where was the first electronic tramway in Europe built?

Q3: What Scotsman became King of Ireland?

Q4: A dispute over the copying of a psalter belonging to Saint Finian by Saint Colmcille led to what famous battle?

Q5: Where was the first Cistercian monastery founded?

Answers:

(1) Tralee (2) Portrush to Bushmills, County Antrim. (3) Edward de Bruce (4) The Battle of Cúl Dreimhne in 561 (5) Mellifont Abbey, County Louth.

The devil will do his best to put you off

Get me to the church on time – advice from a priest

Subtitled 'A Practical Booklet For Teenage Boys', *The Boy's Own* by Reverend T. A. Finnegan was first published in 1957 through the offices of the Catholic Truth Society of Ireland and quickly ran to a second printing. It was circulated in schools, scout halls and churches throughout the 1960s.

A LIFE WORTHWHILE

A soldier must fight. You become Our Lord's soldier in a very special way when you are Confirmed, and you must be prepared to do things, hard things, for Him. His enemies are doing everything they can to wipe out His Church.

If you live reasonably near a Church, the greatest thing you can do is to get up every morning, go to Mass and receive Jesus in Holy Communion. To do that morning after morning calls for great love and manliness.

It will be hard at first and the Devil will do his best to put you off ... but the time will come when the habit of daily Mass and Holy Communion will have grown firm and strong in you, and when you will never allow a lazy, warm bed to hold you from braving the cold morning for One who is waiting on the Altar for you.

Top family films 1966

BATMAN
Starring Adam West, Burt Ward,
Lee Meriweather, Cesar Romero

With West and Ward reprising their small-screen roles as Batman and Robin, this arrived hot on the heels of the wildly successful first TV season. This cartoonish all-actioner opens with the dynamic duo taking to their Batcopter, having received a tip-off that a certain Commodore Schmidlapp is in danger aboard his yacht. As Batman descends on the bat-ladder to land on the vessel it suddenly vanishes beneath him and a highly unconvincing rubber shark bites into his leg. After Batman dislodges it with Bat-shark repellent, the shark explodes. The main plot line is that the United World Organisation's Security Council have been kidnapped and dehydrated, and must be rescued and rehydrated. Their mission accomplished, and world peace restored for now, Batman and Robin exit United World HQ by the window.

BORN FREE
Starring Virginia McKenna, Bill Travers

The reviewer from *The New York Times* summed up the warm, fuzzy embrace that greeted this children's classic from the get-go, writing: 'Almost from the opening shot – a vast expanse of corn-coloured African plain where lions feed on the carcass of a freshly killed zebra – one knows that Joy Adamson's best-selling book has been entrusted to honest, intelligent filmmakers. Without minimizing the facts of animal life or overly sentimentalising them, this film casts an enchantment that is just about irresistible.' Virginia McKenna and her real-life husband Bill Travers star as Joy and George Adamson, who raise the orphaned lion cub Elsa to adulthood. After Elsa is blamed for stampeding a herd of elephants through a village, the couple are given three months to rehabilitate the lioness or see her sent to a zoo. A tearjerker in parts, the circle of life closes with a happy ending.

FANTASTIC VOYAGE
Starring Stephen Boyd, Raquel Welsh, Edmond O'Brien
Raquel Welsh became a star in this sci-fi adventure concerning a team of scientists who shrink, along with their submarine, to microscopic size in order to enter the body of an injured scientist, on a mission to repair some brain damage. The miniature aid team have just one hour to complete their task before the submarine reverts to its full size, with horrible consequences for the patient. The crew are forced to make a long detour through the heart, the inner ear and the lungs, and when their laser gun won't work, they realise that they have a saboteur on board. The baddie meets a sticky end and the others swim to safety via a tear duct in the nick of time. Hailing an instant classic, *Variety* proclaimed it 'an entertaining, enlightening excursion through inner space'. Sticklers for detail continue to ask why the submarine, shipwrecked in the patient's body, didn't return to normal size.

THE FIGHTING PRINCE OF DONEGAL
Starring Peter McEnery, Susan Hampshire, Gordon Jackson, Donal McCann

'A brash young rebel inspires a fight for freedom!' proclaimed the posters for this adventure set in the Ireland of the 1580s. English actor Peter McEnery plays the lead as Red Hugh O'Donnell, the king of Tirconnell, who joins forces with Hugh O'Neill of Tyrone to wage the Nine Years' War against the forces of Queen Elizabeth I. In parallel with playing the role of Kathleen McSweeney in this film, Susan Hampshire was shooting the pilot episode of the classic kids' TV serial *The Time Tunnel* where she featured as a young passenger on the *Titanic* who takes a fancy to time traveller Dr Tony Newman. Playing Captain Leeds, Gordon Jackson would go on to star as the gruff Inspector Cowley in the 1970s hit series *The Professionals*. *The Fighting Prince of Donegal* opened to mixed reviews. It did well at the box office in Ireland, but nowhere else.

THUNDERBIRDS ARE GO
Featuring the voices of Sylvia Anderson, Ray Barrett, Bob Monkhouse

The plot of this TV spin-off revolves around the first attempt to land a manned mission on Mars in the year 2065. However, unknown to the captain and crew, they have an infiltrator on board in the person of the sinister Hood, and the mission ends in catastrophe. As a second Mars attempt is about to be launched, the Thunderbirds team are enlisted to ensure there will be no repeat of the first disaster. The part of this film that attracted most attention and most criticism was a surreal dream sequence featuring puppet versions of Cliff Richard and The

Shadows performing at a space nightclub called The Swinging Star. Cliff pronounced himself 'thrilled' to be part of the Thunderbirds phenomenon. A year before he took the helm at the popular family quiz show *The Golden Shot*, Bob Monkhouse provided the voice of space navigator Brad Newman.

Giving things up for Lent

Good Friday on TV and radio was short and solemn

What are you giving up for Lent?' That was a hot topic amongst children in the schoolyard every spring in the Sixties, and a question put by parents, teachers and clerics which demanded an answer that would meet with adult approval. It was also a matter that got full and sober consideration from a generation of Irish children growing up in a world where Catholic Hell was not just real but waiting to get you.

Each year, just as the stretch in the evenings was making life a little brighter, the Catholic Bishops would read out their Lenten Regulations governing who should do what during the forty days of self-denial that spanned from Ash Wednesday to Easter Sunday. Every newspaper, including *The Irish Times* with its principally Protestant constituency, would give the Bishops' edicts high priority.

The regulations unveiled by Dublin's Archbishop John Charles McQuaid in February 1959 served for the first half of the Sixties with barely a tweak. McQuaid expected nothing less from his flock than supine obedience. Before getting down to the giving-up bit, the Archbishop gave a rap on the knuckles to all those 'heedless' parents 'who, abandoning the authority they hold in sacred trust from God, neglect to control firmly the leisure time of their children'. He elaborated: 'In particular we deplore the unseeing negligence of some parents who permit immature boys and girls to be exposed to the dangerous occasions of sin provided by certain teenage dances.'

Not long after, Archbishop McQuaid opened the 1960s with a challenge to Ireland's doctors and psychologists to come up with a distinctly Irish way of teaching teens about the birds and bees – without going into any gory detail. He reminded them that they had a duty 'to supply instruction in chastity that is accurate, clear, adequate and supernatural' in such a manner as would 'tranquilize the adolescent'.

The Lenten Regulations demanded that all Catholics should offer up the penance brownie points from whatever they gave up, for all those 'suffering persecution for the faith, especially in Communist China'. The Regulations added that every good Catholic should give a wide berth to Communist sympathisers in their community and their 'perverse way of life'.

Children escaped the worst of the giving-up rules. The regulations dictated that Catholics aged between twenty-one and sixty were bound by the laws of fast and abstinence. Fasting meant eating just one meal a day, with an optional light morning and evening snack for the weak and the weak-willed. Abstinence meant no meat. Those between the ages of seven and twenty-one were bound only by the law of abstinence. During the season of Lent 1960 which ran from early March to mid-April, every day was a fast day except Sundays and St Patrick's Day.

While children under seven were exempt under Church law,

and older children were only obliged to give up meat on set days, the culture of the time dictated that every Catholic child should give up sweets, chocolate, sugar or some sweet treat for the duration. Most sweet sellers of the time had at least one collection box on the counter bearing the slogan Penny For The Black Babies, and these filled up over the course of Lent.

The upshot was that Ireland's sweetshop owners looked forward to Lent with even more trepidation than did the nation's children. The Lenten Regulations were lifted for Saint Patrick's Day each 17 March and the sweet sellers relied on the holiday trade for a much-needed spurt of cash flow. In the pre-supermarket age of the early Sixties, the traditional window display was a key advertising prop, and the confectioners' trade mag advised: 'As confectionery events go, St Patrick's Day does not rank with the importance of Easter. March 17th does, however, make a good "filler" display. Green and confections and Irish novelties and favours should be presented amid appropriate surroundings.'

The confectionery Easter egg reflects the ancient association of spring with the start of the laying season, but older folk in the 1960s could recall a time when chocolate eggs were less common than marzipan, toffee and sugar ones decorated with icing. By the start of the 1960s, however, chocolate Easter eggs had virtually wiped out the competition and, with Irish factories lagging decades behind the latest mechanised production techniques, Cadbury's two Dublin plants alone employed almost 3,000 workers making Easter eggs by hand.

In October 1962, two momentous events took place which would each have a profound effect on the lives of Irish children over the course of the rest of the decade. In the space of six days

The Beatles released their first single, 'Love Me Do', and Pope John XIII opened the Second Vatican Council in Rome. A Church defined along hard lines from time immemorial suddenly began to mellow out and the forces of social change, icebound for decades, began to thaw.

One of the first Catholic leaders to see the straws in the wind was the Bishop of Derry and Raphoe, Dr Charles Tyndall, who reached out to bring popular culture into the embrace of traditional Church teaching. As the Weight Watchers organisation was being launched in 1963, Bishop Tyndall argued that there was no good reason why someone going on a diet could not offer up the sacrifice to God. He declared in his Lenten pastoral letter: 'I don't think it is irrelevant or wrong to say we can slim for Jesus Christ. That is simply another way of expressing the spiritual meaning of abstinence.'

Ireland by 1963 was enjoying a mild but giddily unfamiliar economic bounce, and the spiritual reason behind Bishop Tyndall's endorsement of slimming was his fear that the whole notion of self-denial was becoming 'unpopular' as, for the first time, people had money to spend on little luxuries. He urged his flock, children included, to 'review' their 'animal appetites' and cut down on chocolates, butter, sugar, jam, cigarettes and drink.

The Second Vatican Council was wrapped up in December 1965 and Lent in Ireland would never be quite the same again. It's safe to suspect that when Dublin's authoritarian Archbishop McQuaid read out the new Lenten Regulations in February 1966, he did so through gritted teeth. In the early years of the 1960s every day of Lent, bar Sundays and St Patrick's Day, were days of fast and abstinence. From 1966 onwards, days of such extreme obligation would be slashed to just two, Ash Wednesday and Good Friday. Archbishop McQuaid felt that his flock could make up for the lost self-denial in other ways, suggesting: 'This relaxation of the Lenten fast ought to stimulate the faithful to give more generous alms.'

For the children of Ireland, the new Lenten regulations brought especially good tidings. Under the old rules, everyone between the ages of seven and twenty-one was obliged to give up things. Under the new rules, everyone under the age of fifteen could from now on decide for themselves how much, or how little, they would give up for Lent.

***

In 1965 the national broadcaster started its Lenten observance the day before Lent actually began, with a religious TV programme aired at 8.30 p.m. on Shrove/Pancake Tuesday. According to the *RTÉ Guide*: 'This year Lent is of particular importance to Irish Catholics. Not only will we follow the Church's preparations for Easter, but we will enter into a deeper understanding and participation than was possible before.' The centrepiece of this religious observation was a series of ten programmes covering the story of mankind 'from the Fall of our first parents (Adam & Eve) to the Passion and Resurrection of Our Lord ... The history of the Chosen People will unfold before the camera'.

Good Friday TV and Radio 1965

The skeletal TV listings in the *RTÉ Guide* were printed beneath a sombre black masthead featuring the letters INRI plus three nails of the Cross and a hammer. The acronym INRI (Latin: *I sus Nazar nus, R x I dae rum*) represents the Latin inscription which in English reads as 'Jesus the Nazarene, King of the Jews'.

TV Schedule

3.00   *Stations of the Cross*

3.35   *The Way of the Cross* – 'Documentary on Christ's last earthly journey.'

4.30   *Crucified, Dead And Buried*: 'Hymns and meditations.'

Closedown

Radio

2.00   *Devotional Hour For Church of Ireland Listeners*

3.00   Closedown

5.00   *The Passion and Death of Our Lord*

6.20   Interlude

6.30   *News, Weather, Closedown*

GOOD FRIDAY TV 1968

TV Schedule

4.00   *News Headlines*

4.01   *Stations of the Cross*

4.30   *Journey Without God*

5.00   *Death ... And New Life* (meditations and hymns)

5.30   *News*

5.35   Closedown

Could you find me a girl around fourteen years of age?

The genteel childhood hobbies recommended by adults

Published by the Christian Brothers in 1962, the information brochure *Courtesy For Boys and Girls* offered well-intentioned basic advice to children on suitable pastimes. Some of the advice was very, very basic, such as: 'If a concert item is good, show that you like it by clapping.'

The author suggested: 'Recreation, in some form or other, is necessary for everyone, but it should be taken in moderation. Films, television shows, plays and concerts are popular forms of entertainment. Intelligent boys and girls have, however, other interesting pastimes – games, athletics and hobbies such as painting, stamp collecting, photography, cookery, ballet or model-making.'

One pastime encouraged by parents and teachers alike was opening up channels of communications to different lands through one or more pen pals. The Household Budget Inquiry for 1965–66 indicated that the amount spent each year on stationery and postage was enough to be worth keeping track of. Belvedere Bond advertised itself heavily as 'Ireland's finest stationery'. Family publications like *Ireland's Own* devoted pages to those seeking pen pals, while newspapers and children's comics ran weekly contact columns.

In the mid-1950s one Montana schoolgirl in search of a pen pal had bypassed the usual channels and went straight to the top when she wrote to Taoiseach John A. Costello. Addressing him 'Dear Prime Minister,' she ventured, 'This is the first time I have written a letter to a Prime Minister,' so please forgive me if I have made any mistakes in the opening of the letter ... I read in the newspapers that you were in New York for Saint Patrick's Day. Was this the first time? How did you like the country and the parade? ... Could you send me some real shamrock? ... About how many people are there in Ireland? How many square miles in Ireland? What is the largest city? Could you find a girl around fourteen years of age as a pen pal for me?'

The Taoiseach's Department sent young Patricia a booklet on Ireland.

Walt Disney: children's hero, cartoon villain

The dark side of the mogul who played up his Irishness

When Walt Disney died in December 1966, it was if a part of every child's Christmas died with him. For Irish kids of the 1960s, and their parents, Walt Disney and school holidays went hand in hand. By mid-decade, with television fast becoming part of the social fabric in Ireland, Disney's specials were already a centrepiece of the weekend schedules of Telefís Éireann, UTV and BBC. And Walt himself was the kindly, smiling uncle who closed each extravaganza with the reassuring words: 'When you wish upon a star your dreams come true.'

Originally penned for Disney's 1940 classic *Pinocchio*, 'When You Wish Upon A Star' had been quickly adopted as the signature tune for the Irish Hospital Sweepstakes, persuading Irish parents and children that Walt really was family. Walt was fond of stressing his Irishness and crowds of youngsters cheered him when he visited Dublin in person for the world premiere of one of his pet projects *Darby O'Gill and the Little People* in the summer of 1959.

Walt Disney

Disney presented himself to his adoring public as a benevolent genius, loving husband and doting father. Behind the mask there lurked a vindictive, paranoid megalomaniac who inspired dread and loathing in those who knew him best. Decades after his death, he would be occasionally exhumed and debunked as the heartless, grasping Roger Meyers Jr in *The Simpsons.*

Born in Kansas in 1901, Disney endured a harsh, traumatic and loveless childhood. His father, Elias, was a Bible-thumping, child-thumping alcoholic capable of flying into demonic rages. Understandably terrified by this wicked parent, the young Walt would seek refuge in the wishful thinking-up of a better, *real* father elsewhere.

A vague feeling that he might be illegitimate was fuelled when the seventeen-year-old Walt volunteered for army service in the First World War, only to discover that there were no records of his birth. The mystery deepened when the US Department of Vital Statistics unearthed a birth certificate for a Walt born to Elias and Flora Disney. But this Walt's birth date was 1891, which would make him fully ten years older than he'd supposed, which did not seem possible. This bizarre mystery hanging over his origins haunted Disney all his life, but there was to be no even happy-ish ending in the way of closure. The mystery remained to his dying day.

In the light of this conundrum at the centre of his being, it seems no coincidence that Disney's films are awash with themes of parental abandonment or separation. Stepping into the breach is a guardian who is usually either exceedingly kind or excessively cruel. Bambi is separated from both parents; Snow White is an abandoned stepdaughter; the puppet Pinocchio craves the parental approval of Gepetto; Dumbo strives to find his lost mother. Absent parents also feature in *Peter Pan, The Sorcerer's Apprentice, Lady and the Tramp* and a brace of his 1960s blockbusters, *One Hundred And One Dalmatians* and *Mary Poppins.*

Ireland's, and the world's, most beloved family entertainer was, to his own family, a hellish street angel, house devil. After eight years of marriage, his wife Lillian surprised him with the news that she was pregnant. It drove him to distraction. His heavy drinking got heavier, he upped his cigarette consumption to sixty a day, he developed nervous tics and began an obsessive regime of washing his hands once an hour.

Made to feel uneasy and threatened by flesh-and-blood creatures – his wife and children included – he exerted absolute control over his cartoon creations. The term hadn't been coined in the 1960s, but Walt Disney was a control freak. Although full-length animated masterpieces like *Fantasia* and *Dumbo* were long and complex collaborative pieces involving hundreds of top creative talents, Disney shared the credit with nobody. As the Disney legend grew, some of the best and brightest talents in animation remained faceless, nameless and poorly paid.

To his animators, Disney was a charlatan – a moderate draughtsman who lacked the patience and skill to combine images seamlessly. They also viewed him as a tyrannical ogre with an industrial relations policy modelled on Scrooge. Meanwhile, weaving one of his greatest fantasies, Disney worked assiduously to portray his staff of thousands as one big, happy family who whistled while they worked. In this skewed version of things, Walt played the Snow White role, bringing order and good cheer to his corporation's merry dwarfs.

In fact, Disney had more in common with Mickey Mouse than Snow White. Various Irish and British TV packages of Disney's Mickey Mouse Club were a big hit with young Irish viewers during the 1960s, by which time both Mickey and Walt had shared the same startling image makeover. When Disney introduced Mickey to the world in 1928, the rodent was an abrasive street punk – a struggling grifter like his maker. With the coming of sound the following year, Walt lent his own voice to Mickey. As the years passed and Walt cultivated the affection and respect of wholesome Middle America, the mouse was reinvented as a loveable Mickey Rooney character. Minnie was installed as his equally butter-wouldn't-melt Judy Garland sweetheart. As Walt transformed himself into the world's favourite uncle, Mickey became, in the words of his maker, 'a boy scout'.

Disney's employees had no difficulty smelling the rat in their corporation. To mark Walt's thirty-fifth birthday the animators threw a big bash for their boss. The high point of the evening was a raunchy cartoon depicting Mickey and Minnie as they'd never been seen before. According to one biographer, the X-rated short was 'a pointed metaphor for the way they felt they were being treated by Disney, expressed in the act Mickey performed on his girlfriend'.

The birthday boy lived up to his reputation. When the lights went up Walt applauded, said how much he'd enjoyed the jape and asked which members of his fold had been responsible. When the proud perpetrators stepped forward he sacked them on the spot. He then walked out in silence, leaving the stunned revellers to ponder the error of their ways.

Disney sacked his gifted animators at such a rate that they eventually banded together to set up the rival company UPA, which created the great 1960s children's favourite, *Mr Magoo*. A staple of Telefís Éireann's early evening schedules, the near-sighted accident-prone retiree also provided one of the surprise box-office hits of 1962 with *Mr Magoo's Christmas Carol*.

The myth of Disney was not punctured on these shores until long after his death so when he died on 14 December 1966, it really did feel for a great many Irish children that a part of their happy childhood had perished with him.

Top family films 1967

DOCTOR DOLITTLE

Starring Rex Harrison, Samantha Eggar, Anthony Newley, Richard Attenborough

This musical spawned one of Irish radio's heavy rotation airplay hits of the 1960s in the form of '(If I Could) Talk To The Animals' which beat off competition from Dusty Springfield's 'The Look Of Love' from the 007 spoof *Casino Royale* (1967) and 'The Bare Necessities' from *The Jungle Book* to win the Oscar for best song. However, the film itself was not the hit its makers expected. Rex Harrison plays an eccentric doctor who shares his London home with a menagerie of pets, including a chimpanzee and a chatty parrot. The shooting ran way over time and over budget, largely because of the chaos caused by the enlistment of 1,200 live animals, including pigs, birds and giraffes. Before it hit the screens, Irish toyshops and stores were saturated with scores of merchandising tie-ins including Doctor Dolittle talking dolls, pet food and breakfast cereals.

GENTLE GIANT

Starring Dennis Weaver, Vera Miles, Ralph Meeker

Following up on the success of *Flipper* and *Clarence, The Cross-Eyed Lion*, Ivan Tors hit the jackpot again with this big-screen version of the TV series *Gentle Ben*. Like *Flipper*, an unlikely friendship is forged between a small boy and a large animal, in this case an American black bear. Ben the bear is packed off to a zoo after meting out rough justice to a sadistic poacher, but the animal escapes en route and returns to the wild in Florida's Everglades. The boy's father (Weaver) enters the forest intending to shoot the rogue bear, but when a tree falls on the hunter it's up to the gentle giant to free the father and pave the way for everyone to live happily ever after.

THE HAPPIEST MILLIONAIRE
Starring Fred MacMurray, Tommy Steele, Greèr Garson

Former teen idol Tommy Steele plays an Irishman recently arrived in the United States in this lavish affair billed by Disney as 'The Happiest Musical Of The Year!' The young immigrant lands a job as a butler in the household of eccentric millionaire Anthony Biddle, who runs a boxing and Bible school from his horse stables and keeps pet alligators in his study. The real Biddle did keep alligators as pets, and founded a movement called Athletic Christianity, which claimed some 300,000 members at its peak. Steele's big number is 'I'll Always Be Irish' (a claim undermined by his awful Oirish accent), which was written by the Sherman Brothers (who also scored the year's monster hit *The Jungle Book*) in part homage to the late John F. Kennedy and the recently departed Walt Disney, who was fond of parading his Irish roots.

THE JUNGLE BOOK
Featuring the voices of Phil Harris, Sebastian Cabot, Louis Prima

Walt Disney died during the production of this animated classic, but not before he had nixed early versions of the screenplay and soundtrack which stuck closely to Rudyard Kipling's book of the same name. The finished product would be a lighter and frothier variation on the book, better suited to family consumption. The story follows the adventures of Mowgli, an abandoned child raised by wolves, whose world is threatened by the return of the man-eating tiger Shere Khan (George Sanders). Aided by Bagheera the panther and the feckless bear Baloo, he braves the jungle's many perils to make his way to his true home, the Man Village. The film was a huge global hit, with the critics placing it with the Disney studio's finest achievements. Time called it 'thoroughly delightful ... the happiest possible way to remember Walt Disney'.

THE RELUCTANT ASTRONAUT
Starring Don Knotts, Leslie Nielsen, Joan Freeman

Thirty-five-year-old Roy Fleming (Knotts) is the operator of a spaceship fairground ride who lives at home with his parents. He secures a job with NASA as a janitor, but his family believe that he's training as an astronaut. Fired for posing as an astronaut, he is swiftly rehired by NASA, keen to out-do the Russians who are sending a dentist into space. The hapless Roy gets peanut butter into the guidance system and is in danger of being marooned in space. He remembers the retro rockets from his time on the amusement park ride and launches them, bringing the capsule safely home. Following his tickertape reception back on planet Earth he proposes to the woman he loves and the newly-weds settle down to live happily ever after.

Shooting Michael Collins to the moon

First Confession's Frank O'Connor and the Cold War space race

The most critical phrase is between take-off and splash-down.' That was the wry joke of one NASA boffin as Apollo 11 was launched on its perilous and epic mission to put mankind on the moon. By any measure the moon shot of July 1969 was a truly fantastic voyage.

It was a mere dozen years since the USSR had opened a new frontier by putting the football-sized Sputnik satellite in orbit. It was just eight years since President John F. Kennedy, humiliated by the Bay of Pigs debacle in Cuba, had pepped-up his people (and dismayed NASA) with the words: 'I believe that this nation should commit itself to achieving the goal, before this decade is out, of landing a man on the Moon and returning him safely to Earth.'

It seemed an impossible dream, but on 20 July 1969 the human race bonded in communal glory as Neil Armstrong set foot on the lunar surface and declared: 'This is one small step for man, one giant leap for mankind.' Amid the wonderment, no one

dwelled on his omission of the word 'a' (he'd meant to say 'one small step for a man').

NASA's victory in the moon race was won with a devastating sprint down the home straight after lagging behind for most of the contest. The Russians had led with a series of firsts, including first dog in space, first man, first woman, first teams and first spacewalk. In contrast, the US effort had been hampered by doubts, disasters and cutbacks. No sooner had JFK outlined his vision than former President Eisenhower condemned the moon-shot project as 'an expensive stunt' and Congress responded by tightening the purse strings. President Kennedy ultimately roped in a Cork man to support his case.

The long-running Leaving Cert anthology of short stories, *Exploring English*, was first published in the year of the moon landing. For many reluctant readers, by far the best story of the whole lot was 'First Confession' by Frank O'Connor. Although the cheeky 'First Confession' was a delight in itself, its cachet was given a further boost whenever a savvy teacher pointed out O'Connor's special place in the space race.

On a visit to Texas in late 1963, President Kennedy rebuffed Republican calls to slash the space budget for 1964. The *Irish Press* reported: 'Mr Kennedy related the O'Connor story of how as a boy, when he and his companions came to an orchard wall that seemed too high to climb, they took off their caps, tossed them over the wall and then had no option but to follow them. Mr Kennedy said: "This nation has tossed its cap over the wall of space, and we have no choice but to follow it. Whatever the difficulties, they must be overcome."'

The *Press* added: 'Mr O'Connor said last night that he was very pleased to hear that President Kennedy had used this quotation from his autobiography. "I think it is a very brilliant use of the quotation and I would never have thought of it myself," he said.'

The O'Connor quotation was virtually Kennedy's last word on the subject. It appeared in the *Irish Press* the next day, 22 November 1963, the day Kennedy was killed by an assassin's bullet in Dallas.

With Moscow aiming for a landing by late 1967, the US effort seemed doomed that same year after three astronauts perished in a launch-pad fire when Apollo 1 exploded, at a write-off of $80 million, and large chunks of the space budget disappeared into the black hole of Vietnam.

As 1968 dawned, a US moon landing seemed to be drifting ever further out of reach. Mutinous mutterings wafted from Mission Control where the scientists were frustrated by the cancellations and delays caused by cutbacks. One spoke of their frustration watching colleagues in other areas advance in their careers, while the supposed high-flyers of NASA were stuck in a rut.

Tensions emerged between the astronauts and their ground handlers. There were heated arguments between Mission Control and the crew of Apollo 7 who all had colds, and were plagued by runny noses. They wanted to leave their helmets off during landing so they could blow their noses. The controllers said no. The sniffling astronauts won out. During another exchange, the Apollo 7 commander sent word that when he returned he'd like to step outside with "the idiot" who'd devised unscheduled tests which were sprung on the exhausted spacemen.

But if 1967 and 1968 were fraught, by the start of 1969 all systems were go and Ireland wanted its piece of the action.

A special copy of a NASA film of the Apollo 7 mission was secured and shown to hundreds of schoolchildren at the RDS, watched over by Foreign Affairs Minister Patrick Hillery. A year before the landing a new Waterford firm, Torison Balance, went to work on a super-sensitive weighing scale to be used to weigh and parcel the moon dust and rock collected by Apollo 11. With an eye on the big farming readership, Irish newspapers stressed 'Apollo's Flight Will Be A Help To Agriculture'. Reports said that surveillance of crops from space would soon help spot the appearance of diseases and parasites at an early stage.

There was surprise when NASA passed over more experienced astronauts to name the crew for the moon landing as Neil Armstrong, Edwin 'Buzz' Aldrin and Michael Collins. The *Kilkenny People* urged pride in the latter's 'famous Irish name' while all the papers noted that his mother was a Finnegan from Lissinaskea in Mayo. With the Vietnam War shedding support by the day, the lone civilian Armstrong was given command in what was seen as a sop to gathering popular hostility to US participation.

Not everyone was happy with Armstrong's leadership role, including, reportedly, Buzz Aldrin. Two weeks before lift-off a former NASA official revealed that, as pilot of the lunar landing module, Aldrin was intended from the outset to be the first man on the moon. He'd even practised his exit manoeuvres for his moment of immortality. Instead, Armstrong had exercised his 'commander's prerogative' and 'bumped' Buzz down the line. Aldrin's father, a retired colonel, bit his lip and told reporters that 'all that counts' was that America got there before the Reds.

In May 1969 Apollo 10 made the final test flight, chalking up a number of firsts, including one that has a profound effect on daily life for men today. Astronaut Tom Stafford told Earth: 'All three of us shaved today using a very new technique called shaving cream and a razor, and it worked beautiful.'

As Apollo 11 prepared to launch, the Japanese delegation to a UN conference on outer space called for the speedy signing of an international liability agreement to cover death and damage caused by space junk raining from the sky. Nothing was signed.

On the weekend of 20 July 1969 the people of Ireland watched and waited as the lunar module detached from the orbiting spaceship and attempted the risky landing.

As the descent began, Armstrong and Aldrin discovered to their dismay that they were passing mapped landmarks on the surface four seconds early. They sent back word that they were 'long' and would have to land miles from their target spot on the Sea of Tranquillity. Their luck held and they somehow landed safely on a rock-strewn patch with only seconds of fuel to spare.

After they completed their landing routine, Buzz Aldrin's first act was to dispense himself the sacrament of Communion with some sanctified bread he'd brought along. It had to be a private act because at the time NASA was fighting a lawsuit brought by a US citizen who had objected to the crew of Apollo 8 reading from the Book of Genesis, and who argued there was no room for religious practice in space. Putting down his marker on the issue, President Richard Nixon attended a White House service to pray for a successful mission, where the offending passage from Genesis was made the centrepiece. To this day, Aldrin's church, Webster Presbyterian in Texas, commemorates the first Lunar Communion on the Sunday nearest 20 July.

As the first grainy pictures beamed back from the landed craft, the one-in-seven earthlings with access to TVs rejoiced, apart from those in the USSR who were grudgingly informed at the end of the Saturday night film. The Soviet TV service finally broadcast a seven-minute clip of the moon landing at 10 a.m. the next morning when, as one Irish paper noted, 'relatively few people were at home'. Meanwhile, next door in Red China the people weren't told at all.

JFK's inspirational speech had stressed 'returning them safely to Earth' and the world waited with bated breath for news of a successful lift-off. This part was not televised. NASA cited technical reasons but many believed it was just in case the worst happened. Happily it didn't. Unhappily for the Kennedy family, the fulfilment of JFK's dream kept every other story off the front pages apart from the one they desperately did not want to see there. That lone story spoiling the party featured a photo of a young woman called Mary Jo Kopechne and the headline 'Died In Kennedy Car'. At the very instant JFK's status as a saintly visionary was sealed, the career of younger brother Teddy was cast into the murk by a woozy escapade that cost his young passenger her life.

President Richard Nixon, beaten to the White House in 1960 by JFK, was receiving detailed updates on Teddy's troubles as he stood by to speak to the astronauts moments after they planted the Stars & Stripes on the moon. The President had prepared a long speech for what he described as 'the most historic phone call ever made from the White House'. He was persuaded to scrap his lengthy speech and keep his contribution short by a NASA liaison officer who told him that any perceived attempt to elbow in on the Kennedy legacy would lose him votes.

After two-and-a-half hours on the surface, the two astronauts climbed back aboard the lunar module and prepared for the most dangerous part of the whole mission. If the craft failed to blast off and dock with Collins in orbit, they would be marooned and doomed on the scene of their great triumph. The module lifted off with just one tiny hitch – the blast from the ascent rockets flattened the US flag they had planted. Future landing crews would be instructed to plant the flag a lot further away.

That night, as Apollo 11 sped homewards, the men, women and children gathered in Dublin's Whitefriar Street Church, hushed as visiting US Bishop Fulton Sheen offered up a special prayer he had composed. It captured the spirit of the triumphal day, and the mind expanding decade of Flower Power and *Star Trek*, saying: 'Everything in the Universe is man's … Man must bring the Universe under his subjection … Man has got the Earth into his head, now he must get the Heavens into his head by understanding and mastering them.'

In Jordan, recently mauled by US-supported Israel in the Six-Day War, the moon landing marked a sinister development, with its leading newspaper warning that the US would use moon bases to obliterate unfriendly parts of the Earth, giving kids yet one more thing to worry about. The Greeks, taking a sunnier view, declared a national holiday.

The next day, bookies William Hill paid out lavishly to a Preston man who, in 1964, had taken their odds of 1,000/1 that man wouldn't walk on the moon by the end of the decade.

His £10 wager had earned him £10,000 or over two years' wages. William Hill said they'd learnt their lesson and wouldn't underestimate the space racers again. They opened a new book, offering the much more sensible odds of evens on man walking on Mars by 1979.

MOON LANDING TONIGHT

For the children of Ireland, as in many other parts of the world, 20 July 1969 was Christmas in the middle of the summer holidays. The placards of street vendors shouting 'Heddled-o-Press' proclaimed 'Moon Landing Tonight'. The primary-school holidays were three weeks old, but some leftover learning lingered in the nation's young minds. Geography lessons had taken a swerve from sugar beet in Tuam to safe moorings on the Sea of Tranquillity. For months every teacher had been able to reel off pat answers on weightlessness, splash-downs, quarantine, and whether space bugs could invade Earth.

***

After a decade of relative prosperity and calm, unease had invaded Ireland. Marching season in the North was simmering to boiling hatred. Industrial disputes were erupting daily. Republicans burned out the homes of German and English farmers in the south, shaming and upsetting local communities.

Against this, the moon landing was a feel-good thing. Above all, it was about the kids. Most were allowed stay up late to watch *The Virginian* on Telefís Éireann, followed by brief coverage of the actual landing around 9 p.m. Then it was up to bed with the promise of a 3 a.m. wake-up for the moonwalk.

The older folk stayed on to watch Telefís Éireann's big film *The Bank Dick* starring W. C. Fields (1940). Telefís Éireann's coverage of the main event had a gaping hole in the middle.

Those who could get BBC or ITV did better, with the latter mounting a seven-hour showbiz extravaganza around the landing. For the very few with colour sets, BBC2 was the only service broadcasting in colour. When the bleary kids were roused at 3 a.m., many found the real thing far less impressive than *Star Trek*. (Kirk & Co. bubblegum cards were the hot schoolyard swap that year.) Following the movements of Armstrong and Aldrin was like trying to track two ghosts in a snowstorm, but there was something memorable about being up watching telly at such an unearthly hour.

Sitting there dunking biscuits into hot chocolate, no one could have faintly imagined that just two years later the public would become so jaded that NASA would have to pay the TV stations to cover the Apollo 17 mission.

A–Z

T

Terry Wogan After his hit TV quiz show *Jackpot* was dropped by Telefís Éireann, an opening arose in 1967 for Terry Wogan to join the starting line-up of the BBC's new pop station, Radio 1, as the host of *Late Night Extra*. A star was born.

Tomorrow's World During the heightened Cold War of the 1960s presenter Raymond Baxter told viewers of the BBC science show, in all earnestness, that the Russians had drawn up an action plan to make contact with approaching aliens before they reached Earth, in order to get to them 'before they can be contaminated by the capitalists'.

Tranny The popular term for a transistor radio.

Tupperware Party Plastic Tupperware containers were heavily marketed for keeping food fresh and as school lunchboxes. The ladies-only Tupperware party was a gathering in the home of the party-giver, whose aim was to demonstrate and sell the Tupperware range to friends and neighbours while everyone had a good time.

TV Detector Van First unveiled in these islands in England in 1952, these roving crime labs were allegedly capable of uncovering TV sets in households with no licence. Kids were fascinated and a little intimidated, but the abiding suspicion – seemingly confirmed in a 2013 UK report – was that they were a con job perpetrated by the authorities.

Twix The two-fingered Twix was launched in the Summer of Love, 1967, when The Beatles, Rolling Stones and the Flower Power generation were giving a different sort of two fingers to the Establishment.

U

Urneys Chocolate
Based in the Dublin suburb of Tallaght, the Urney chocolate factory employed some 3,000 workers at the start of the Sixties, rolling out some of the nation's favourite lines, including Rovals, Beanos and the extra-wide Two & Two bar which was a multicoloured, multilayered delight combining dessert and milk chocolate, cream fudge and vanilla fondant.

Crumbling teeth & celebrity tonsils

The average ten-year-old had six teeth missing, decayed or filled

The Irish Girl Guides' Toothbrush Song
(To the air of 'O My Darling Clementine')

Little Mary had a toothbrush,
and she hung it on the wall.
Did she use it? Did she use it?
Did she use it? Not at all.

Then one morning at the table
She began to scream and shout:
'Oh! my Mommy, I've a toothache!
Will I have to get it out?'

Mommy took her to the dentist,
and the dentist shook his head:
'It's too late for little Mary.
She should have brushed her teeth instead.'

The agreed cure between the medical profession and the general public for recurring tonsillitis in the 1960s was to whip them out and put an end to the matter. Children were put under the knife more readily than today, and the prevailing wisdom was that the young came out of the whole business suffering far less pain than adults.

By 1960 the surgical solution had become such an orthodoxy that Professor R. A. McNeill of Belfast's Royal Victoria Hospital warned a faddish general public not to be seduced by celebrity tonsillectomies. Professor McNeill published a paper that year entitled *A History of Tonsillectomy: Two Millennia of Trauma, Haemorrhage And Controversy*.

He concluded: 'Like many other operations, tonsillectomy waxes and wanes in popularity. The eagerness with which the lay public advocate tonsillectomy for all manner of complaints has undoubtedly led to unnecessary operating. Also, from time to time, some prominent citizen undergoes tonsillectomy and the consequent publicity leads to a spate of operations on the tonsils.'

Staying in the region of the same bodily orifice, the children of 1960s Ireland dreaded a visit to the dentist almost as much as a trip to the hospital to get their tonsils out, and not without reason.

By the dawn of the decade the nation's teeth were in a shocking state of disrepair. The desperate solution for a great many adults was to have the derelict husk of their ivories extracted and a set of dentures fitted. One of the great aspirations shared by most Irish parents of the 1960s was that their children would grow up to have a set of teeth they could proudly call their own.

At the start of the decade the state's action plan to combat rotten teeth in children consisted of little more than 'a special leaflet on oral hygiene and the prevention of dental caries', plus two short films on dental decay entrusted to the National Film Institute's Mobile Units which showed up once in a blue moon at schools across the country. Health Minister Sean MacEntee acknowledged that this was hopelessly inadequate to the task but as he told the Dáil: 'Dental decay is so widespread among school children ... that it is beyond the resources of health authorities, in funds and dental personnel, to cope with this grave problem by treatment alone.'

A few years earlier a top dentist had told the press: 'If all sweetshops were prohibited by law then the dental surgeon's work with children would largely disappear.' This was clearly never going to happen, of course, but the Health Minister did have a cunning one-size-fits-all plan. To confirm that the dental decay was as bad as he feared, he ordered a survey of 27,000 children in the cities of Dublin, Cork, Limerick and Wexford, and the counties of Kildare and Wicklow. It established that in Dublin and Cork the average ten-year-old had six teeth missing, decayed or filled. Worse, Irish teenagers had to negotiate their crucial snogging years with one third of their teeth blighted or gone. However, the survey singled out one glistening oasis of fresh-breath confidence. In the village of Patrickswell in County Limerick, said the report: 'Fluorine is naturally present in the public water supply. In this village the children's teeth were markedly healthier than elsewhere.'

Legislation approving the fluoridation of water supplies had been passed in 1961 but a body calling itself the Pure Water Association had stirred up an effective poisoned-well scare. The Pure Water lobby charged that fluoridation amounted to an unwarranted 'mass medication' capable of producing untold horrors. More than half a century later, the reasoned arguments of the Pure Water Association resurface from time to time, as Ireland remains one of the very few European countries to practise fluoridation. With the issue in the balance, all objections to the scheme were dismissed as the paranoid imaginings of a lunatic fringe.

Pushing ahead with his scheme to fluoridate the country's drinking water, Minister MacEntee put it on the record that there were only two possible alternatives to his plan, and that both were clearly impossible. One would be to treble the number of dentists in the state to 1,800 at huge cost. Apart from the expense, it would take years to train 1,200 extra dentists and the country's 600 existing practitioners would fight tooth and drill to preserve their highly lucrative closed shop.

The other alternative to fluoridation would be to improve people's eating habits and dental hygiene. The Irish were now rivalling their British neighbours as the biggest sweet eaters in the world, and mountainous dollops of refined sugar were stirred into tea, porridge and anything else that would bear sweetening. Propaganda efforts such as 'The Toothbrush Song' drilled into every Girl Guide were making little impression – toothbrush sales were dismal.

Ruling out the practicality of getting people to take better care of their teeth, Minister MacEntee argued that the Irish poor mouth was an inevitable by-product of progress. His twelve-page government information pamphlet explained: 'The fundamental cause of bad teeth is the modern diet – and this is something that cannot be changed substantially. Ireland is no exception here: all advanced countries must pay the penalties of the modern diet and none has found a way of changing either the diet or the habits of eating, least of all among the children.'

The clincher for the Minister's bold plan, he insisted, was that it was cheap, but fuming away on the opposition benches, Fine Gael's Richie Ryan was passionately against adulterating the nation's supply of pure water. The Minister's report, charged Ryan, was an unscrupulous effort 'to push fluoridated water down the throats of an unsuspecting public'.

The chief battleground was the capital itself, and Dublin Corporation held a heated debate over whether to support or oppose the Health Minister's sweeping proposal. When the vote was called, Richie Ryan howled at those about to vote in favour that they would 'be counted with the murderers of the children of Dublin' by future generations.

His impassioned cry was to no avail. The fluoridation measure was passed by a margin of twenty-five votes to fifteen. Dubliners' teeth, and then the nation's, began to improve dramatically despite a sharp rise in sweet eating, while water-related deaths remained largely confined to drownings.

Enthused by its victory in the fluoridation battle, the state stepped up its campaign to bring the war against rotten teeth into every home and school in the land. By 1967, the last week of October had been dubbed Dental Health Week. While lectures and film shows took place in hundreds of schools, the Army Dental Service targeted mothers with a seminar in Dublin's Mansion House. The government was delighted to report that after an intensive six-month tour of remote rural schools and their disadvantaged inner city counterparts, the country's first Mobile Dental Clinic had got the nation's children smiling that bit brighter.

Top family films 1968

CHITTY CHITTY BANG BANG
Starring Dick Van Dyke, Sally Ann Howes, Lionel Jeffries

Based on the novel of the same name by 007 creator Ian Fleming, and produced by the man behind the Bond films, Albert Broccoli, this musical also featured Gert Frobe aka Auric Goldfinger as would-be car thief Baron Bomburst. Maverick inventor Caractacus Potts (Van Dyke) converts a wrecked racing car into a marvellous creation that is equally adept at sailing the high seas and flying high as a kite. Potts, his two children, and his sweetheart Truly Scrumptious (Howes) foil the various attempts of the evil Baron to steal their magical car, and when Potts manages to sell the invention of musical Toot Sweets to Truly's industrialist father, the inventor is now in a position to propose marriage to her. *Time* called it 'a picture for all ages, the ages between five and twelve', but it became a huge box-office hit.

"Chitty Chitty Bang Bang"

FINIAN'S RAINBOW
Starring Fred Astaire, Petula Clark, Tommy Steele

Fred Astaire came out of retirement at the age of sixty-nine to play the part of Finian McLonergan, a chancer who skips

Ireland with a crock of stolen gold in his carpetbag. He arrives in America convinced that if he buries his gold close to Fort Knox it will multiply. In hot pursuit is a leprechaun by the name of Og, who will turn into a human if he doesn't get his gold back. All manner of magical mishaps take place, most notably when a racist white senator is turned into a black man. Performed by Petula Clark, the film's slushy showpiece song, 'How Are Things In Glocca Morra?', became a staple fixture of Irish radio. Tommy Steele's hysterical impersonation of a leprechaun was roundly condemned as one of the worst cases of stage-Oirishness ever witnessed but the film was nevertheless a hit.

THE LOVE BUG
Starring Dean Jones, Michele Lee, David Tomlinson
Dean Jones headed the bill as washed-up racing driver Jim Douglas in this Disney flower-power-on-wheels vehicle, but the undoubted star for millions of enchanted small children was Herbie the Volkswagen Beetle with a mind of his own. An unlikely friendship develops between Douglas and the Beetle after the driver intervenes in a row between the car and an evil showroom dealer called Peter Thorndyke. Much of the film is taken up with Herbie's efforts to make a match between Jim and Carole Bennett (Lee), but when they finally go on a date the sneaky Thorndyke takes the opportunity to nobble Herbie by pouring Irish coffee into his tank. It all ends happily with Herbie whisking Jim and Carole off on their honeymoon.

OLIVER!

Starring Ron Moody, Oliver Reed, Harry Secombe, Mark Lester, Jack Wild

The winner of six Academy Awards including Best Picture, this musical adaption of Charles Dickens' novel swept all before it at the box office. Ron Moody shone as the deeply unlovable rogue Fagan, and Oliver Reed gave a tour de force as every child's most feared screen villain, Bill Sikes, but it was sixteen-year-old Jack Wild who stole the show as the Artful Dodger. He was discovered by the theatrical agent mother of one of his footballing teammates, Phil Collins, later to find global fame with the band Genesis. On the back of *Oliver!*, Wild would land the star role in the hit kids' TV fantasy series *H. R. Pufnstuf* which screened in the US in 1969 and was a big favourite in Ireland during the early 1970s.

YELLOW SUBMARINE

Starring The Beatles, Lance Percival, Dick Emery

The 1966 Beatles song 'Yellow Submarine' was already a favourite singalong at children's parties when this full-length animated feature appeared. Paul McCartney rejected attempts to read any deep meaning into his lyrics, saying: 'There's nothing more to be read into it than there is in the lyrics of any children's song.' In the film, Sergeant Pepper's Lonely Hearts Club Band must protect the undersea paradise of Pepperland from the onslaughts of the music-hating Blue Meanies. The Fab Four eventually prevail over the Blue Meanies' fearsome weapon, the Dreadful Flying Glove, by singing 'All You Need

Is Love', and the Chief Blue Meanie sees the error of his ways. Peace breaks out and both sides of the dispute join together in a big party with everyone belting out a rendition of 'It's All Too Much'.

When you grow up I want you to be ...

The role models that parents and teachers tried to foist on their children, and the ones the kids chose themselves

The role models that parents and teachers tried to impose on their children were a far cry from the ones the children decided upon themselves.

With Telefís Éireann about to take to the airwaves on the last day of 1961, Ireland's Social Study Conference convened that year for its annual summer school. The theme of the event was The Challenge of Television. One of the challenges for Irish society, the delegates agreed, was to ensure that the new medium provided proper role models for the boys and girls of Ireland, especially the girls.

One speaker stated that: 'A feminine ideal is a necessity for young girls and the absence of any regular "heroines" on television screens [is] injurious to young girls, especially teenagers. Serial features on women heroines such as Elizabeth Fry, Edel Quinn, the Angel of Dien Bien Phu, or some of the valiant women of the Old Testament could be attractively presented and should contain enough drama to satisfy even male as well as female viewers.'

Elizabeth Fry was a devoutly Christian social reformer popularly known in her time as The Angel of Prisons. Edel Quinn was a crusading Irish missionary who spread the word of Christianity through East Africa. The Angel of Dien Bien Phu was Geneviève de Galard, a French nurse who saved countless lives with historic distinction during the 1950s war of independence between the Vietnamese and their French overlords. It was role models of this calibre, with seemingly not a frivolous bone between them, who were held up by the parents of Ireland to their boys and girls as the type of person they should hero worship and want to be like.

But the world was changing fast, and the speakers at the Social Study Conference were quite astute in identifying television as the single biggest influence on whom Ireland's boys and girls would hero worship, and what they'd most want to be when they grew up. But when it came to a choice between wanting to be a valiant woman of the Old Testament or Batgirl, there was only ever going to be one outcome.

Role Models For Girls – What Parents wanted

Jackie Kennedy

For most of the 1960s, when Irish mothers dressed their little girls in their Sunday best, those little girls more often than not were decked out like miniature Jacqueline Kennedys, sometimes right down to the Chanel-type suit, the pillbox hat and faux-pearl necklace. Early on, Jackie had it all. She was beautiful, stylish, a doting Catholic mother whose people came from Cork, and who was married to President John F. Kennedy. She was loved by Ireland as the First Lady, and doubly so for her dignity and courage following his murder. In 1968 she shocked the world when she married shipping magnate Aristotle Onassis to become Jackie O. It cut little ice with Irish parents that he'd provide the privacy and security she craved for her children.

VIRTUES: Many, then none.

Bernadette Greevy

Parents, teachers and clerics all loved Ireland's finest mezzo-soprano who made her professional singing debut in 1961 as Maddalena in the Dublin Grand Opera Society's *Rigoletto*. By the mid-1960s she was an established recording star, with one *New York Times* review commenting: 'The voice has the firm compact resonance of a true contralto. She has endless breath and can move her voice with agility and precision.' Resisting calls to move to a bigger music metropolis, she based herself in Dublin, remarking: 'If you're good enough you can live where you like.' Every parent's role model for their little girl, she was showered with honours including Malta's Order of Merit and the Papal Cross.

VIRTUES: Great job, class act, Papal approval.

Edel Quinn

Declared Venerable by the Vatican, Edel Mary Quinn (1907–1944) was a lay missionary who worked with distinction in

Africa. Born in Cork, she was called to a religious vocation at an early age. Her first instinct was to sign up to the Poor Clare order, but advanced tuberculosis put an obstacle in her path. In her late teens she joined the Legion of Mary, becoming one of that body's most committed activists. Her work in helping to clear the most notorious slums of Dublin marked her out, and in the late 1930s she expanded her horizons, and her good works, to Africa. Despite persistent tuberculosis, she extended the reach of The Legion of Mary across East Africa.

VIRTUES: A tireless worker with great faith.

Granuaile

Queen Medb of Connacht was a greater warrior, but was far too earthy to be role-model material. Granuaile, aka Gráinne Mhaol or Grace O'Malley (1530–1603), was born into a great seafaring family with trading links that stretched from Spain to Scotland. After her first husband died in battle, she married Richard, who was chief of the Burke clan in Mayo. She was captured while on yet another piracy raid on English ships, by the Earl of Desmond in 1577. A year in prison did nothing to quell her habits and she returned to her career as a Gaelic pirate upon release. Her raids were a consistent thorn in the side of English rule.

VIRTUES: She really annoyed the English.

Julie Andrews

For many Irish parents, Julie Andrews throughout the 1960s could be summed up in a single line that she delivered as Mary Poppins, having delighted her young charges with her magical measuring tape. That line, of course, was: 'I'm practically perfect in every way.' After winning the hearts of the nation's kids in *Mary Poppins*, Andrews nailed the gig as the world's most wholesome entertainer as the loveably problematic mountain-climbing nun Maria in *The Sound of Music*. More Mom's apple pie in 1967's *Thoroughly Modern Millie* left *The Irish Times* queasy, but she could yet do no wrong with Ireland's parents.

VIRTUES: Practically perfect in every way.

Lady Augusta Gregory

The gun-totin' firebrand of the 1916 Rising Constance Markievicz was possibly more admired by parents, teachers and elder lemons, but she was too bolshie and had left her husband. Born into the same Protestant Ascendancy, Augusta Gregory moved from Unionism to Nationalism and took a key role in the birth of a new, independent state. She co-founded The Abbey Theatre, writing a number of works for it, and was a central figure in the movement known as the Irish Literary Revival. Her motto was deeply patronising, but at least she borrowed it from Aristotle: she said that it was vital 'to think like a wise man, but express oneself like common people'.

VIRTUES: Abandoned Unionism for Nationalism.

Saint Brigid

The fact that Brigid started out as one of Ireland's top pagan goddesses wasn't so much glossed over in the 1960s as known to few. As far as parents and teachers were concerned, she was the Queen of Christian Ireland and lesson one in many primary arts and crafts classes was how to make the Saint Brigid reed cross, familiar as the logo of Telefís Éireann. Scholars recognised it as the ancient pagan Sun Cross, or Wheel Cross, associated with Taranis, the God of Thunder, who became the Roman god Jupiter. The multitasking Brigid of pre-Christian lore was Ireland's weather deity, while her post-Christian self changed her bathwater into beer for serving to visiting clerics.

VIRTUES: Hardworking housewife material.

Anne Devlin

Anne Devlin was born in Wicklow into a family deeply committed to the struggle for Irish nationalism. Moving to Dublin, twenty-year-old Anne met Robert Emmet. Emmet's revolt in 1803 was an abject failure. What was planned as the capture of Dublin Castle, the strongpoint of British rule in Ireland, became a street skirmish. Anne, as his loyal and loving co-conspirator, was amongst the first to be rounded up, along with members of her family. She was tortured but refused to provide evidence against Emmet, although her bravery did not save his life. Anne Devlin lived on for almost a half-century after her release from jail, but it was not a happy life, and she died in penury.

VIRTUES: Stood by her man and Ireland.

Mary O'Hara

If there was a pecking order of role models that 1960s parents would press most ardently on their young daughters, Mary O'Hara might win hands down. Gifted with a beautiful soprano voice, and a dab hand on her trademark harp, she bewitched audiences in Britain, America and the world. Tragedy shattered her enchanted existence in 1957 when her husband of fifteen months died of Hodgkin's disease. She continued to tour and record, but in 1962, still grief-stricken, she became a

Benedictine nun and entered Stanbrook Abbey in England. At the close of the decade, that was where her heart-rending, inspirational story stood. (She would later resume her career and remarry.)

VIRTUES: Grace under pressure.

ROLE MODELS FOR GIRLS – WHAT KIDS WANTED

One of the Four Marys

In 1953 the Pope ordained that 1954 would be the first Marian Year in the long history of the Catholic Church, leaving many pious parents who didn't already have a daughter named Mary to rectify that situation. The data of the Central Statistics Office shows that the spike in Mary-naming continued right through the 1960s, topping the charts throughout the decade. The upshot was a strong identification amongst a big chunk of Ireland's girls with the cover stars of the most popular girl's comic, *Bunty*. Much like the later Spice Girls, girls could identify with the Mary of their choice – Mary Field, Mary Cotter, Mary Simpson or Mary Radleigh.

VIRTUES: Weekly adventures with lashings of ginger beer.

Batgirl

Batgirl Yvonne Craig was mobbed when she arrived at Shannon Airport in 1967 for a promotional visit. With colour television still some years away in Ireland, viewers couldn't appreciate Batgirl's purple-and-yellow caped outfit nor her purple Batcycle with its white lace trim – at least not until the Batgirl doll and her accessories fetched up in Irish toyshops. Batgirl provided freelance assistance to the daring duo of Batman and Robin in the camp TV show that proved a huge hit with Irish boys and girls. By day, Batgirl was the prim librarian daughter of Commissioner Gordon.

VIRTUES: Superhero daughter of Gotham's Irish police chief.

Darrell Rivers from *Mallory Towers*

Throughout the 1960s, as was the case in previous decades, there were no Irish comics and almost no books which held up a mirror to the lives of junior Irish readers. The result was that, for all the fierce attempts of Official Ireland to impose, inflict or otherwise encourage a total immersion in 'Irishness', nature abhorred the vacuum and kids turned to British comics and books. In the context, approved role models like Saint Brigid or Lady Gregory were never going to hack it against posh public-school girls always getting into scrapes, like surgeon's daughter Darrell Rivers from Enid Blyton's boarding school series.

VIRTUES: Smart, loyal, trustworthy but not to be messed with.

Samantha from *Bewitched*

While no Irish boy wanted to grow up to become a bumbling advertising executive like Darrin Stephens (or Derwood, as his interfering mother-in-law Endora dismissively called him), just about every little girl wished she could become a nice, middle-class witch like the ever-resourceful Samantha. The hapless Darrin was forever falling victim to some evil spell or other, and Samantha's weekly task was to twitch her nose until the world had been put right again.

VIRTUES: Pure magic.

Helga from *The White Horses*

Only thirteen episodes of this Yugoslavian–German co-production were ever made, but from the time they first appeared on Irish and British television in 1968 they were on heavy rotation for years. Countless Irish girls wished themselves into the role of Julia, a youngster from the big smoke of Belgrade who spends a wonderful summer of adventure on the stud farm of her uncle Dimitri, where she takes a fancy to dishy groom Hugo, but really falls in love with the white horses of the title. In the English-language version, the memorable and enduring theme song was sung by Dubliner Jackie Lee.

VIRTUES: She could talk to the animals.

ROLE MODELS FOR BOYS – WHAT PARENTS WANTED

John F. Kennedy

He was young, he was handsome, he was dashing, he was the most powerful man on Earth and he was one of us. Born into a large American family that was proud to call itself Irish, the son of Prohibition-bootlegger-turned-US-Ambassador Joe Kennedy, JFK was a blue-blooded role model before his thoughts ever turned to running for the White House. His Second World War exploits as the heroic commander of the motor torpedo boat *PT-109* were turned into a film that became a box-office hit in the summer of 1963 as the President made a triumphant visit home to the land of his forefathers. Kennedy's assassination just months after his

Irish visit piled martyrdom on sainthood, and not a bad word would be heard.

VIRTUES: All of them.

Eamonn Andrews

A formidable balance of brain and brawn, Dubliner Eamonn Andrews lifted the Irish junior middleweight boxing title before setting his sights on broadcasting. Radio Éireann was soon too small to hold him and he set forth for the BBC, which fell to his charms in no time at all. In addition to becoming Britain's favourite sports commentator, he found fame as the host of TV's *What's My Line?* and even hit the Top Twenty with a 45 rpm single produced by George Martin. And while their parents admired him, Ireland's kids (who could get the BBC) loved him as the genial host of *Crackerjack*, the Friday teatime show that signalled the weekend was here.

VIRTUES: Dads wanted to be him. Mams wanted Dad to be him.

John Wayne

His ancestors were Presbyterians from Antrim and his closest living relationship to Ireland was probably his bond with his favourite Hollywood director John Ford, whose parents hailed from Spiddal in County Galway. But even before he arrived in Mayo at the start of the 1950s to shoot Ford's *The Quiet Man*, glamour-starved Catholic Ireland had adopted John Wayne as one of their own. Wayne was a man's man who always fought on the side of right, and Irish boys needed little encouragement from their fathers to want to grow up to be just like him. Comically stage Oirish as it was, The Duke's barn-storming performance as Sean Thornton demonstrated to young boys that you could be a violent drunk and still cool.

VIRTUES: Being John Wayne.

Padraig Pearse/James Connolly/Éamon de Valera/ Michael Collins

Well into the 1960s one of the abiding Irish stereotypes was that the typical living room would have on the wall three images – Jesus Christ, the Pope, and Éamon de Valera. While this was sometimes the case, the Civil War of forty years past was still an open wound and many parenting couples kept their politics to themselves. When role models came up for discussion, the deeply Catholic Pearse and socialist Connolly were often set up as alternatives, while Dev and Collins were pitted more – to use a despised modern phrase – as nerd v jock. For the purposes of commemorating the Golden Jubilee of the Easter Rising in 1966, Pearse got the nod over all comers.

VIRTUES: Bravery and a love of Ireland.

Tony Dunne

A week after winning the FAI Cup with Dublin club Shelbourne FC, the unassuming Dunne signed for Manchester United in 1960. A small and compact full-back, Dunne was quick in the tackle, even quicker to recover, and was equally hard to get past on either flank. By the close of the decade Tony Dunne had earned a place as a bona fide United legend in the great side of Best/Law/Charlton. He helped the team to an FA Cup (1963), two English League titles (1965, 1967), and had an outstanding game as Matt Busby's team defeated Portuguese kingpins Benfica to lift the European Cup in 1968. In 1969 he was voted Irish Footballer of the Year.

VIRTUES: Modesty, dependability, work rate.

Matt Talbot

Not the most glamorous of role models, this unfortunate Dublin labourer was nevertheless held up to boys and girls as someone to consider and admire. Born in the 1850s into a family of heavy-drinking men, his poor job choices (a wine merchant's, followed by a whiskey depot) led him astray early. A hopeless alcoholic at thirteen, he took the pledge in his late twenties and spent the final four decades of his life sober. Talbot took as his own role models the early Irish monks, subjecting himself to a regime of fasting, prayer and, as became evident when he died, wearing chains beneath his clothes. While kids weren't expected to go to his extremes, they were invited to find him inspiring.

VIRTUES: Hmmm …

Christy Ring

The 1960 inter-county hurling year kicked off with the sport's most famous veteran still going strong. Cork's Christy Ring had won his first All-Ireland winner's medal fully nineteen years earlier, followed by three more in a row, and the nation expected that he would hang up his boots at the close of the 1960 championship season. The same story played out in 1961 and 1962, before the legend stepped down from top-class hurling at the age of forty-three. Ring's scoring prowess was the stuff of legend, and he retired with an unheard of eight All-Ireland winner's medals to his name. Beloved of GAA fans and Christian Brothers everywhere, he was held up to young boys as the man with the right stuff.

VIRTUES: Skill. Endurance.

Edmund Ignatius Rice

The founder of the Christian Brothers moved from Kilkenny to Waterford City in the 1770s where the number of hungry waifs begging on the streets troubled him deeply. He made his fortune as a chandler, supplying goods to ships, but tragedy struck when his pregnant young wife, Mary, was killed when she was thrown from her horse-drawn coach. Instead of wallowing in his grief, Rice sold up his business and opened a school for poor boys. In association with the Bishop of Cork, Rice began training up a band of Christian Brothers to carry the flame of knowledge from Waterford to the world.

VIRTUES: A love of learning and helping the poor.

Hugh O'Neill

Presented to Irish schoolboys as The Great O'Neill, the Earl of Tyrone fought the last major rearguard actions of Gaelic Ireland against the conquest of Elizabeth I. Following a spectacular victory at the Battle of the Yellow Ford midway through the Nine Years' War, defeat at the Battle of Kinsale spelled the end for the last outposts of autonomous Gaelic Ireland. O'Neill and his ally O'Donnell fled Ireland for Spain in 1607 with a large entourage of lesser chieftains and camp followers. The so-called Flight of the Earls would leave a power vacuum which would be swiftly filled by a strengthened English administration and the plantations of large numbers of Scots and English colonists.

VIRTUES: Moral victories and an actual one.

Daniel O'Connell

Every schoolboy and schoolgirl was taught to admire Daniel O'Connell for the way he gave Ireland's cruel British rulers a bloody nose, by taking on the English in their own Parliament and forcing them to concede Catholic Emancipation in 1829 and subsequently by attracting huge numbers (100,000 on average) to what became known as Monster Meetings, rallies at which he spoke in favour of repealing the Union of Great Britain and Ireland. The other, darker side to O'Connell's character was probably not so much airbrushed out by teachers, as untold to them too. Only in a later Ireland would 1960s schoolchildren learn that the Great Liberator doubled as the Great Fornicator. A hothead and a bully forever picking fights, O'Connell settled one row with Dublin Corporation by shooting dead one of its members in a duel.

VIRTUES: Catholic Emancipation in 1960s Ireland scored 10/10.

Role Models For Boys – What Kids Wanted

Batman

In the early 1960s Batman was known to most Irish boys from the higher-up magazine racks of the country's bigger newsagents. He was important enough to have his own DC comic, but compared to *The Victor* or *The Sparky*, these

American imports cost too much pocket money and had far too few strips. But Batman came in from the cold with a vengeance from 1967, when a camp, colourful caped crusader burst onto Irish TV screens, answering the call of the police Batsignal projected onto the clouds, being left to die at the close of each cliffhanger ending, and always somehow getting free to win the day. Every young boy wanted to grow up to drive a Batmobile and go to work in a superhero costume finished off with a utility belt, the Swiss army knife of belts.

VIRTUES: All of the above.

James Bond

Sean Connery first came to the notice of Irish children when he played the lead role in Disney's 1959 fantasy *Darby O'Gill and the Little People.* Connery's character spent that film engaged in a battle of wits against leprechauns, to general indifference. But when he pitted those wits against the evil SPECTRE in the first two James Bond films the world sat up and paid attention. Connery's brooding 007 was instantly the world's best secret agent and a role model every bit as appealing as Batman. Like the enforcer of Gotham City, James Bond had all the best gadgets, drove the best car, and got to have fun while killing baddies in the name of goodness.

VIRTUES: Licensed to kill.

George Best

The young Sean Connery was a useful footballer and the future star related that the legendary Matt Busby tried to sign him for Manchester United in the mid-1950s. Connery turned down Busby on the grounds that a football career would be too short.

George Best did, however, sign for Busby, and in the course of the 1960s became the James Bond of the football pitch. He had all the cool of 007, drove the best cars, got the best girls, and was given the roving licence to kill off oppositions as he saw fit. While Bond famously derided The Beatles in *Goldfinger*, the moptop Best was hailed by the Continental press as *El Beatle* after a one-man demolition of formidable Lisbon side Benfica in 1966.

VIRTUES: Played the Beautiful Game beautifully.

Jai from Tarzan

While the young boys might aspire to grow up to be the Tarzan of the 1960s television series, for the moment they'd generally settle for being his young orphaned sidekick, Jai. The fabled apeman and his entourage were retooled and repackaged for the grandchildren of cinemagoers who'd been thrilled by the exploits of Johnny Weissmuller's Tarzan and his Roscommon-born Jane, Maureen O'Sullivan. Played by Ron Ely, Tarzan was now an urbane, highly educated city slicker who, as was fashionable in the age of Flower Power, dropped out of the rat race to rediscover the jungle where he lived as a boy. Jane and son Boy were jettisoned, reducing Tarzan's regular companions to the cheeky chimp Cheeta, and Jai, an Asian waif somehow abandoned in the heart of Darkest Africa. None of that really mattered, because Jai never once had to recite the *tuiseal ginideach* or rattle off the eleven times table.

VIRTUES: He got to live in the jungle and hang out with monkeys and Tarzan.

Will Robinson

Set in the distant future of 1997, the hit TV show *Lost In Space* followed the adventures of the Space Family Robinson, selected from 2 million volunteers as the first unit of mother, father, son and daughters to colonise deep space. They were accompanied by the shifty saboteur Dr Zachary Smith and the clunky robot handyman B-9. The villain of the piece, Smith, was also the star of the show, always up to some mischief that puts the entire mission in jeopardy. While the robot and pilot Major Don West always kept a watchful eye on the slithery Smith, trusting son Will Robinson would always give him the benefit of the doubt. Despite Will's naivety, he enjoyed the perfect life, boldly going where no ten-year-old boy had gone before.

VIRTUES: His home was a spaceship.

A–Z

V

Val Doonican Rocks, But Gently. In March 1967 the Waterford musician, famous for performing in a rocking chair, knocked The Beatles' *Sergeant Pepper's Lonely Hearts Club Band* off the top of the UK album charts to become the first Irish artist to have a Number One LP there.

View Master Projecting holiday slides onto the living room wall was a favourite way of entertaining guests and relatives, but for solo viewing of slides 'in stereo' the View Master promised 'the world at your fingertip'.

W

Waiting in line Waiting for things was an inescapable part of life in a country that wasn't firing on anything like all cylinders. There were long queues to the counters of grocery shops, in the post office, outside the local phone box, everywhere.

X

X-Ray Specs The glossy and pricy imported Marvel and DC comics from the US carried a number of regular adverts that ran issue after issue for years on end, firing the imagination of Irish youngsters who were dismayed that they couldn't order these marvels without dollars and some deeply exotic and mysterious thing called a Zip Code.

Y

Yodel Chocolate Spread For Bread 'A well-known dietician says that the average spread of Yodel, on bread or butter, gives growing children 50% more energy than bread and butter alone.' Perhaps, but Yodel's stay on Irish shop shelves didn't make it to the 1970s.

Yuri Gagarin Every Irish schoolchild knew this Russian cosmonaut's name after he became the first man in space in 1961, and shared a twinge of sadness when he was killed in 1968 when his training jet crashed.

Z

Ziffel The full name of the pig that starred in the beloved US sitcom *Green Acres* was Arnold Ziffel. Arnold was the surrogate son of childless couple Fred and Doris Ziffel who were the Hooterville neighbours of Oliver and Lisa Douglas.

Zoo For 100 years up to the mid-1960s, in times of very cold weather, the Dublin Zoo authorities would open their frozen lake for ice skating, for a small fee. The winter of 1963 proved to be the last of the skating jamborees.

Knock-knees, flat feet and bat ears

From the parental advisory guide *Your Children's Health – From Two To Twelve Years*

The following pearls of wisdom have been gleaned from the Parental Advisory Guide *Your Children's Health – From Two To Twelve Years,* published by the *Children's Britannica* in 1964.

Bat Ears

A marked degree of bat ears is embarrassing, particularly to boys who cannot cover it with their hair. Strapping with plaster is no good, but this minor deformity can be corrected by plastic surgery if it worries the child.

Round Shoulders

Abnormal postures in children, especially round shoulders, are usually symbolic of their state of mind and sergeant-major tactics can, therefore, only make things worse. The best way to deal with round shoulders is to find a way of increasing the child's self-confidence, usually by finding something that he is good at and encouraging him to pursue it. In adolescent girls, round shoulders are often the result of a desire to conceal their developing breasts.

Pigeon Chest

Pigeon Chest (protruding breast bone) may be inherited from a parent. If the deformity is extreme surgical correction may be necessary.

Knock-Knees and Flat Feet

This is not such a disastrous affair as some shoe manufacturers would have us believe, and often corrects itself as the child grows older. Nevertheless, it can be a handicap, especially for a dancer or athlete, and is best corrected  early on before it becomes a fixed deformity. This is best done by the fitting of a plastic heel seat inside the shoe.

Small children and sweets

Shifting shopping habits bring the two closer

There are competing claims for the title of Ireland's first true supermarket, including a 5,000 square foot H. Williams outlet on the capital's Henry Street (1959), a Dunnes Stores 'personal choice superstore' on nearby South Great George's Street (1960) and the sprawling Superquinn (then plain Quinn's) that incorporated the old Casino Cinema in the Dublin suburb of Finglas (1965).

By the close of the decade, supermarkets, as we more or less know them today, were springing up across Ireland, transforming the shopping experience for the nation's kids from a drudge of getting dragged from pillar to post to a fun excursion.

For mothers – and it was nearly always mothers – grocery shopping before supermarkets required patience and planning. For the children who got dragged along, it was a grim purgatory of hand-holding, filing in line along dull counters and wondering how on earth your mother could find so much to discuss with all the neighbours. Filling a single shopping basket might involve popping into the grocer, greengrocer, newsagent, butcher, fishmonger, haberdasher and chemist.

Many items were shelved behind a broad counter that you couldn't properly see over and your mother had to point and ask for every single thing she wanted. Cash registers were rare, sliding wooden drawers common. A receipt would consist of totted sums on a scrap of brown wrapping paper.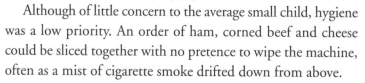

Although of little concern to the average small child, hygiene was a low priority. An order of ham, corned beef and cheese could be sliced together with no pretence to wipe the machine, often as a mist of cigarette smoke drifted down from above.

The coming of the supermarket changed all that. From a child's vantage point of three feet tall, they were a maze of aisles you could get lost in, stacked with a variety and colour never before gathered in one place, and a ceiling so lofty you could fly a kite, if you had a kite.

No sooner had Superquinn's Feargal Quinn laid his claim as the founder of this transformation operation than he was joined by Leitrim-born Pat Quinn, recently returned from Canada and bringing with him a splash of showbiz that no youngster could resist. In 1966 Pat opened his first Quinnsworth store in Stillorgan and for small children it was nothing less than an adventure park. Perched in a booth like a demented motorsport commentator, the proprietor would bark out news of special offers and great cash giveaways over the speaker system.

Fergal Quinn once recalled that when his father opened Ireland's first proto-supermarket, in Dundalk, customers didn't fully grasp the concept of the mesh shopping baskets provided. He said: 'My father came down to see the shop a few hours after it opened and as he was walking up the street he saw people with our baskets. He said to them he didn't think they were meant to take them out of the shop, and people were genuinely amazed they had to leave them at the door.'

Supermarket shopping in the 1960s was a different experience from today, in ways that have receded into the mists of time. There were no barcodes, pesto or fizzy water. There were no loyalty cards. Instead, customers would receive sheets of Green Shield stamps, which they would give to their children to stick into the books. The stamps could be used to redeem gift items like kettles and toasters from depots around the country. Credit cards were something you generally only saw in Bond films. Happily, there were no known vegetarians in Ireland, since vegetarian options were cabbage and spuds and suchlike, and were to be eaten with liberal servings of meat.

What Feargal Quinn and Pat Quinn had in common was that they transformed the relationship between small children and sweets. Before the coming of the big supermarket, a parent with a kid or kids in tow would go to the butchers to buy meat and to the vegetable shop for greens. In either place there was no prospect they'd end up having a standoff over sweets.

But there was no way of escaping the new one-stop supermarkets without having to negotiate the rows of sweets, chocolate bars and lollipops stacked in front of each till. And with the supermarkets came another American brainwave for selling more sweets to more people – bigger bars split into more squares and, later, the family pack of bite-sized pieces

The confectionery industry in the US had hired the sales guru Ernest Dichter to help them boost sales. Dichter is credited with dreaming up the term 'focus group' and the Esso slogan 'Put A Tiger In Your Tank'. At a time when low-calorie sugar drinks were getting a heavy marketing push in the States for the first time, Dichter identified guilt as standing between the shopper and the sweets on display.

To combat this guilt, Dichter came up with the concept of 'self-indulgence in moderation'. He reasoned: 'You will be providing the excuse the customer needs to buy a bar of candy – "After all, I don't have to eat all of it, just a bite and then put the rest away." – Seriously, we doubt whether the rest will be put away. However, the consumer will be left with the feeling that candy manufacturers understand him and the bite-size pieces will give him the "permission" he needs to buy the candy because the manufacturers are going to "permit" him to eat in moderation.'

The advent of the supermarkets coincided with the signing of a new Anglo-Irish Trade Agreement in 1965 which led to a flood of new sweets onto the Irish market. The agreement came about after the French blackballed Ireland and Britain from joining the European Economic Union (EEC) in 1963. The Dublin government saw the need to shed Ireland's protective wall of import duties in readiness for another attempt to join the Common Market.

The new supermarkets were now free to stock up on sweets and bars which Irish viewers had seen advertised on British channels for years but which had been kept out by high import duties.

Speaking in the Dáil in 1968, the Labour TD Michael O'Leary complained that the supermarkets were using imported sweets and biscuits to draw in customers, while the money spent was now leaving the country. He charged: 'Up and down the country there are neon signs, and supermarkets which … have their own interests in mind first. They push their own business interests, they push their own manufacturers and their own British wholesalers. Only last week I ventured into one of those commercial temples. I noticed they were pushing British biscuits, British cheese, British confectionery and so on.'

A short time earlier, the Dáil had debated another worrying new trend in confectionery – the chocolate bars were getting smaller. Labour's Dr John O'Connell asked the Minister for Industry & Commerce George Colley if he was aware 'that many manufacturers, as well as increasing the price, are reducing the size of the product?'

The Minister agreed that this was happening, but there was nothing he could do about it. The supermarkets brought a mixed bag of changes, but all things considered, for the kids it was mostly all right.

The brainchild of schoolboys on Christmas vacation

The battle to keep young Irish ears safe from foreign pop music

In Ireland of the 1930s, 1940s and 1950s, recorded music was confined almost entirely to the living-room wireless set which was a clunky device that couldn't be moved from the sideboard because its glass valves were so delicate. Better-heeled homes would have the wireless built into a sideboard, which would also house a gramophone player and a couple of shelves for the 33 rpm discs made from vinyl or heavy shellac. From the early 1960s the type of music kids could hear changed dramatically, along with where and when they could hear it.

The only source of music was locked into the living-room wireless or gramophone and access was firmly in control of the parent who might want to listen to a talk programme, or some light classical music, or nothing at all. Two new arrivals at the start of the 1960s gave Irish teens and children remarkable new freedoms. The playing of records was liberated from the living room by the advent of the Dansette record player. Just a basic turntable in a box, these light and portable players could accommodate seven-inch 45s, ten-inch EPs, and twelve-inch long-players, or LPs. The Dansette brand was pricy, but it spawned a host of cheaper copycats for which many teens could save.

When records migrated to the bedroom, away from the controlling parental hand on the dial, teens and their younger siblings could play the music that spoke to them, be that The Beatles or Pinky & Perky. But the bedroom was just the opening point of a musical generation gap between kids and parents that would end the decade as a yawning chasm. With the advent of the transistor radio, popularly called the 'tranny', the consumption of pop music moved out of the bedroom and into the great outdoors.

The tranny was pioneered by the Tokyo Telecommunications Engineering Corporation in the mid-1950s. By the early 1960s, with both the device and eventually the company now recognisable by the Sony logo, the transistor radio was in the process of revolutionising music. Cheap, light and portable, the tranny was also robust because the fragile vacuum tubes of the old sets had been replaced by a miniature transistor-based circuit board. Now that pop music could be accessed on the bus, in the car, in the park, on the beach, night and day, the pop industry stepped up several gears to meet the fantastic new demand. New record labels started up, new bands were signed, and new pirate radio stations mushroomed in Britain and Ireland.

Irish kids and teens took a certain pride in the fact that the biggest and best of the pirates of the mid-decade was the brainchild and plaything of an Irishman. In March 1964 swashbuckling young Ronan O'Rahilly took to a life at sea, launching a venture he named Radio Caroline after the daughter of the recently murdered John F. Kennedy. Anchored just outside Britain's 3-mile limit off the south of England, the non-stop pop station was an instant hit with a youth fed up with the meagre music rations provided by the stuffy BBC. Caroline quickly became a game changer, providing a launch pad for acts like The Who and The Yardbirds who were deemed too unruly by the BBC.

Anchored much closer to Dunkirk than Dublin, Caroline was never more than a nice idea for Irish youngsters, whose access to pop music was restricted to the night-time broadcasts of Radio Luxembourg, which were subject to severe atmospheric warping, and the fitful youth output of Radio Éireann. Run by civil servants for civil servants, as it so often seemed, the sole national radio service opened each weekday morning at 8 a.m. with news and weather. There followed two hours of light opera, country 'n' Irish, and elevator music, followed by closedown at 10 a.m. after just two hours on air. The station reopened at 12.55 in the afternoon with another news bulletin followed by a sponsored programme at 1 p.m., the most popular by far of which was *The Kennedys of Castleross* which aired on Tuesdays and Thursdays. While middle-aged, middle-of-the-road tastes were more than generously served, the general rule was that the pop idols of Ireland's children should be not seen and not heard.

And when the pop hits of the day were heard on the national broadcaster, there was often something not quite right about them. This was often because, instead of the station playing the original by The Stones or The Hollies, they would patriotically substitute a hastily recorded cover by one of Ireland's myriad showbands. Although, in truth, this substitution wasn't always done for purely patriotic reasons. Looking back on the period, one impresario remarked that most of the records played on the radio were played through 'little gifts'. The showbands hired people to promote them in that way.

The top showbands were highly paid to be human jukeboxes faithfully reproducing the hits of the day from Britain and America. In order to keep up with the ever-changing hit parade, the bands had to rehearse new material virtually on a daily basis. The wealthier outfits fitted modified Dansette record players, with sprung suspension, into their coaches so they could listen and learn as they travelled the rocky highways and byways. Lower down the food chain the musicians would have to content themselves with listening in to the Radio Luxembourg Top Twenty on Sunday nights in the hope of catching the gist of the new entries.

The showbands ruled the roost of the Irish ballroom circuit and kept the heavily rationed radio and television pop content well clogged up with inferior covers. And when the genuine articles did pop over to Ireland, it was usually to play as guests on Telefís Éireann's weekly *Showband Show*. The *RTÉ Guide* plug for one edition of *The Showband Show* in 1965 listed the guest stars as 'The Tremelos, Freddie and The Dreamers and The Beatles'. When The Rolling Stones arrived in Ireland that same year for shows in Dublin and Belfast, Mick Jagger bluntly told one reporter: 'I don't like Irish showbands.' But the showbands were just about the only show in town, and after their sell-out gigs in the Adelphi Theatre, the Stones found themselves at a party thrown by the Royal Showband.

There, drummer Charlie Watts cheerfully admitted: 'Today was a rave, man.'

Telefís Éireann's alternative outlet for pop music mid-decade was *Pickin' The Pops* presented initially by Gay Byrne and then by Larry Gogan. Larry would subsequently go on to host a radio show called *Mystic Nylons* featuring 'pops-a-plenty'. The *Pickin' The Pops* panel passed judgment on new releases from top acts including, said the advertisements for one 1965 instalment, 'Cilla, The Rolling Stones, Dusty Springfield, Jim Reeves, Elvis, Cliff, The Beatles and Manfred Mann'. Mistrustful of youth culture, the Montrose authorities decided that if they were going to have a pop show, there should be a responsible adult somewhere in the room, and so, in 1965, the *RTÉ Guide* was delighted to report that *Pickin' The Pops* had recruited a new member for its judging panel. He was middle-aged academic Denis Franks, 'professor, revue artist and lecturer in Shakespeare'. According to RTÉ's in-house magazine: 'While we know what he thinks of Hamlet in a Saville Row suit, it should be interesting to hear his comments on Gerry and The Pacemakers, The Kinks and sundry other kings of the waxing world.' By way of balance, another new addition to the panel was twenty-year-old model Imelda McManus.

One rising star of the showband scene vented his frustration with the same scene during an appearance on *Pickin' The Pops* in early 1965. The Impact were sharing the bill on the show with The Young Shadows, a Dublin showband that churned out cover versions of The Shadows. The Impact were supposed to play the downbeat Buddy Holly number 'Valley of Tears', but when the moment came, they launched into a gritty rendition of the Larry

Williams' R 'n' B classic 'Slow Down', on the signal of their rebellious guitarist Rory Gallagher. The panel and the programme makers were taken aback, but there was nothing they could do but let the band play their angry racket.

Rory Gallagher was not the only one who felt it was high time the showbands were put out of everyone else's misery. At the end of the same year, 1965, Gay Byrne looked back on a flat year in Irish pop. He wrote: 'Two years ago the novelty of having our own Irish showbands on disc was so great that the fans rushed out and bought them regardless. It didn't really matter what the song was like or the arrangement or the production. They were our own and they wanted, and got, our support. But now the honeymoon is over.

'They won't buy it any more just because it's home-produced. If you don't deliver the goods they'll go for something better. And what of all the rumours that Irish showbands were "about to break" on the British record scene? A few of them got their chance, took it, and that was the last we heard of it.

'I have gone through the experience every Tuesday for the past three months at the BBC trying to select at least one Irish showband record to include in a record programme. There were very few of them I could honestly stand over.'

Not once during the decade, but twice, a bunch of schoolkids decided to challenge the paucity of pop on the national broadcaster, and the practice of having original hits laundered through the showband mafia. In both cases the authorities moved swiftly to crush these green shoots of youthful rebellion.

In 1964 a group of Cork schoolboys set up their own pirate station called Radio Juliet. The newcomer broadcast the latest original pop hits in the middle of the morning, when Radio Éireann took a nap, and returned in the afternoons with a selection of classical waxings. The music, chat, news and weather could be heard for a radius of around 10 miles from the centre of Cork. The authorities had for decades been quick to stamp out pirate broadcasts by subversives, and were not going to tolerate schoolboy insolence. After the pirate had been up and running for some days inspectors from the Department of Posts & Telegraphs demanded police action, and as a search warrant was being drawn up the pirates decided to abandon ship.

When it was all over several of the boys, who had been using on-air aliases from Shakespeare, spoke to the press. Explaining that they'd built their own transmitter for 6 shillings, one said: 'We feel that there is a desire for more hours from Radio Éireann, so we decided to put on our broadcast in the mornings and afternoons, when Radio Éireann was closed down. We had looked into the legal aspect, as well as the Geneva Convention. We decided to operate on the 210 medium wave, not to interfere with Radio Éireann.' Reiterating the point that they were moved to action by Radio Éireann's needless morning and afternoon naps, the speaker concluded: 'Now that we have successfully operated this station … we intend to seek an interview with the Minister.'

The boys explained that they had run their station on a budget of £1 per day, which included the cost of telephone calls and petrol money. The petrol was to keep their studio mobile. As one explained: 'Our lookout reported that cars with detection equipment had drawn up outside the first site. We quickly moved somewhere else.'

Three years later, as 1967 neared its close, the pop content and opening hours of the national broadcaster still went nowhere near matching the demands of Irish youngsters. As the school holidays began a few days before Christmas another pupil-driven pop pirate went on air, this time in the capital. *The Irish Times* reported: 'Radio Jacqueline appears to be the brainchild of schoolboys on Christmas vacation and yesterday's "pop" music programmes were interspersed with greetings from the announcer to schoolfriends. The transmissions also featured excerpts from the satirical magazine *Private Eye*.'

According to the newspaper, the deejay had unapologetically told listeners that if they wanted news bulletins they should move the dial to Radio Éireann. He signed off with the promise of another 'raving session' of chart hits the following day: 'However, a spokesman for the Department of Post & Telegraphs warned that engineers were investigating the broadcasts and should track the pirates down soon.' With the law on their trail, the schoolkids melted away to spend Christmas at liberty with their families.

Amongst the acts more likely to be heard in the original versions on Irish radio were The Beatles, who famously proclaimed 'We're Irish!' and could boast an army of Irish family ties, The Bachelors who hailed from Dublin, Waterford's Val Doonican and the queen of blue-eyed soul, Dusty Springfield.

Born Mary Isobel Catherine Bernadette O'Brien to Irish parents in London, she attended convent school there and briefly toyed with the idea of signing up as a nun, but music was to be her true vocation. A year after leaving school Mary O'Brien sent shockwaves through the convent by returning, barely recognisable, as Dusty Springfield. Reflecting on her operation transformation, she said: 'I was destined to become a librarian at that point. I had awful glasses, unstyled hair and thick ankles. One day I went to Harrods and came back with this black dress on, and my hair had been done in French rolls, with endless pins in it. I just suddenly decided, in one afternoon, to be this other person who was going to make it.' And make it she did, spectacularly. She went global in 1963 with her first hit, 'I Only Want To Be With You', and became one of the key singles artists of the decade.

While Dusty Springfield was the nun-that-got-away, Jeanne Paule Deckers was the real nun that captivated Ireland's parents, teachers and children when she topped hit parades around the globe with her nursery-rhyme style 'Dominique'. Upon joining the Dominican Order in her native Belgium, Deckers took the name Sister Luc-Gabrielle, but it was as her pop persona, The Singing Nun, that she took the world by storm. Such was her phenomenon that in 1965 Debbie Reynolds starred in a Hollywood biopic of her life, entitled simply *The Singing Nun*.

Even with the pop charts overflowing with Catholic nuns, and Irish-born middle-of-the-road crooners, as well as top acts happy to rejoice in their Irishness, some people just would not be pleased, including members of the Cashel branch of the Irish cultural group Cumann na Phiarsaigh. In 1966, just days after unidentified republicans had blown up Nelson's Pillar in the middle of Dublin, four Belfast schoolteachers dashed into a studio and recorded a cash-in track 'Up Went Nelson' to the tune of 'John Brown's Body'. Within a week or so, schoolyards the land over were filled with the strains of boys and girls singing: 'Up went Nelson in old Dublin / All along O'Connell Street the stones and rubble flew / As up went Nelson and the pillar too.'

As the recording by The Go Lucky Four hit the top of the Irish charts, the state responded by slapping an ill-defined blanket ban on 'rebel songs'. This ban was deplored at the annual meeting of Cumann na Phiarsaigh in Cashel. Chairman Labhras Ó Murchú objected: 'We are subjected to an overdose of pop drivel and duplication and triplication each day, and now the so-called national broadcasting station has taken a step which can only indicate an organised opposition to Irish ballads.'

Until the end of the decade the big problem Ireland's kids and teens had with the national broadcaster was that it played far too many Irish ballads and not nearly enough pop drivel.

***

Best known later as the nation's top sports anchor, Jimmy Magee began the 1960s as Ireland's top pop picker. In 1962 Magee was doing publicity for some of the country's top show-bands when he pitched the idea of an Irish Top Thirty to Radio Éireann. Looking back to a time when broadcasting was largely a matter of making it up as you went along, he much later recalled: 'They said who's going to do it? And I said I'll do it. Between the request shows, distributors' figures and shop sales I compiled it.' The first Irish pop chart appeared in October 1962 and, to the delight of its compiler, the first chart topper was his hero Elvis with 'She's Not You'.

Another young man of the 1960s, Shay Healy, threw more light on the business of putting together a chart in an era when the Irish music business was run on a frequently haphazard basis. Healy's job at *Spotlight* magazine involved compiling the weekly Irish Top Twenty. He recalled much later: 'I never took money to bend the truth, or the charts. You had to bend the charts anyway because you'd never have the figures. You tended to favour the people you liked.'

Two years after setting up Ireland's first official pop chart, in his capacity as the music writer for the *Spar* housewives' magazine, Jimmy Magee made the following prediction: 'I've no doubts Cliff Richard is here to stay. So too are Cilla Black, The Beatles, Ray Charles and The Bachelors. And I'd like to think The Migil 5 as well.' As things stood at the end of the decade, his score was a very respectable five out of six.

IRELAND'S TOP 10 SINGLES, CHRISTMAS WEEK 1964 (COMPILED BY RADIO ÉIREANN)

1 'I Feel Fine' – The Beatles
2 'Down Came The Rain' – Butch Moore and The Capital Showband
3 'Just For Old Times' Sake' – Dickie Rock and The Miami
4 'Walk Tall' – Val Doonican
5 'Distant Drums' – Sean Fagan and The Pacific
6 'I'm Gonna Be Strong' – Gene Pitney
7 'There's A Heartbreak Following Me' – Jim Reeves
8 'Pretty Paper' – Roy Orbison
9 'Boolavogue' – Tommy Drennan and The Monarchs
10 'I Ran All The Way Home' – Brendan Bowyer and The Royal Showband

(Five of the Top Ten were cover versions by Irish showbands.)

Top family films 1969

RING OF BRIGHT WATER
Starring Bill Travers, Virginia McKenna

The male and female leads of *Born Free* were reunited for another nature romp, this time revolving around the antics of a hyperactive otter. The adventure begins when Graham Merrill (Travers) spots a frisky otter in a pet-shop window. Instantly smitten, he makes an impulse purchase and brings the playful creature home. It quickly becomes clear that a bathtub in a poky London flat is no place for Mij the otter so Merrill decides to move to a small village in Scotland and fulfil his dream of being a writer. He and the otter explore the countryside and befriend Mary MacKenzie (McKenna), the kindly village doctor, and her dog Johnny. Tragedy strikes the group but just as it seems there's no happy ending in sight, not one turns up but four. Merrill abandons his attempts to pen a novel about the Marsh Arabs, and finds fulfilment writing about otters.

BUTCH CASSIDY AND THE SUNDANCE KID
Starring Paul Newman, Robert Redford, Katharine Ross

The posters for this classic western proclaimed 'They're taking trains, they're taking banks, and they're taking one piece of luggage!' Based loosely on the true story of Wyoming's Hole In The Wall gang, the film followed the dynamic duo of Butch and Sundance as they blazed a trail from the United States to Bolivia, pulling off a string of daring robberies along the way. When they get to Bolivia the partners in crime try to go straight, but their first honest job as payroll guards goes horribly wrong and the mere notion of settling down to a life of farming or ranching has no appeal. They return to a life of crime, but the Bolivian police track them down and corner them. The film closes with one of the most famous shots in film history, as the daring duo meet their end in freeze-frame.

HELLO, DOLLY!

Starring Barbra Streisand, Walter Matthau, Michael Crawford

Directed by screen legend Gene Kelly, this musical is set in 1890s New York where the shrill widow Dolly Levi (Streisand) is a socialite who offers her services as a matchmaker. Her latest clients seeking assistance are the crotchety 'well-known unmarried half-a-millionaire' Horace Vandergelder (Matthau) and a young artist named Ambrose who is in love with Horace's niece, Ermengarde. The plot thickens when Dolly sets her sights on making Horace her next husband. After a roustabout of comic thrills and spills, the half-millionaire realises that Dolly really is the one for him. He proposes and Dolly gets her man, an outcome that was never in any doubt. Louis Armstrong reprised his 1964 number one hit, taken originally from the Broadway musical, in a cameo. Despite a put-down by *The New York*

Times which said it 'inflated the faults (of the stage production) to elephantine proportions', the film was a huge hit.

KES
Starring David Bradley, Lynne Perrie, Brian Glover

Ken Loach's acclaimed drama focuses on Billy Casper (Bradley), a tormented working-class boy who is bullied both at school and at home. Even his own mother dismisses him as 'a hopeless case'. The son of a single mother (Perrie), Billy's life is bleak until he develops an interest in falconry and begins training a kestrel that he finds on a nearby farm. As the relationship between Billy and Kes, the kestrel, improves during the training, so does Billy's outlook on life. For the first time he can remember, he receives praise, which comes from his English teacher after delivering an impromptu talk on his relationship with the bird. The film was a slow-burning hit in Britain and Ireland, but it flopped in the US where audiences couldn't understand the thick Yorkshire accents.

SUPPORT YOUR LOCAL SHERIFF!
Starring James Garner, Joan Hackett, Walter Brennan, Bruce Dern

The Wild West frontier town of Calendar springs up almost overnight, when the dizzy Prudy Perkins (Hackett) strikes gold in a freshly dug grave during a funeral. Calendar descends into lawless anarchy, with successive sheriffs swiftly dispatched to a plot on Boot Hill. Enter the urbane Jason McCullough (Garner) who insists he's only passing through on his way to

Australia, but displays a special gift for law enforcement. Quicker on the draw than any of the ruffians terrorising the townsfolk, McCullough defeats the bandit Danby clan and marries Prudy. As the film closes, we discover that McCullough will never make it to Australia but will land the coveted post of governor of Colorado.

That summer in Dublin, Kerry, Cork & Donegal

Lourdes, Lourdes, Lourdes, the Holy Land, or, most probably, a staycation

The term wouldn't be coined for decades to come, but the only type of summer holiday known to the vast majority of Sixties Irish children was the staycation. Going abroad was vastly expensive, with a package fortnight in Spain in 1966 eight to ten times the cost in real terms as the same holiday in 2016. As the family car began to appear in more and more driveways, a jaunt to Dublin, Cork or Shannon Airports became a Sunday treat for many, but a wander around the viewing deck on the airport's open roof was as close as most kids, or their parents, ever got to boarding a plane.

One of the mainstays of the Irish travel industry throughout the 1960s was the pilgrimage, most often to Lourdes in southern France, followed by the Eternal City of Rome and, for those with the deepest pockets or the greatest faith, the Holy Land in the Middle East. In 1965 the Dublin-based World Travel Service offered a 'fifteen-day all-inclusive tour of the Holy Land with priest leader' for 139 guineas (a guinea was £1 and one shilling) with an optional excursion to Lourdes. Many

Irish holidaymakers opted for just Lourdes at 36 guineas, availing of 'weekly departures with priest leader'. French Railways Ltd were advertising directly into Ireland, attempting to lure pilgrims with their state-of-the-art 'Wired For Sound' service. The sales pitch boasted: 'Certain pilgrimage trains are fitted with Public Address systems. Live speech and recordings can be broadcast throughout the train by prior arrangement.'

In an age of brown suits, grey concrete and black-and-white TV, one of the great enticements of the foreign holiday was colour. To showcase the blue skies, azure seas and golden sands of Spain, Italy and beyond, Joe Walsh Tours invited the general public each spring to the Hibernian Hotel on Dublin's Dawson Street for free screenings of brightly flickering promotional films for *la dolce vita*. Even in the days long before the package holiday came within reach of the average Irish family, the Irish tourist bar was an established part of the holiday landscape.

In 1965 broadcaster Gay Byrne joined the pioneers of Irish sun travel, taking a Viscount propeller plane to Barcelona and onward by coach to the seaside resort of Sitges. While Byrne loved his stay for the good weather, he questioned the sanity of going all that distance just to spend every night opposite the apartment in a pub call Paddy's Bar where Irish holidaymakers sang ballads into the early hours. He remarked: 'There were big harps on the wall and signs that said things like "*Tir Gan Teanga, Tir Gan Anam*" (a land without its language is a land without a name), and "*Leabhar Gaeilge Anseo*" (Irish spoken here) and "The Border Must Go" and so on.'

For the vast majority of Irish kids of the Sixties, the only Irish pubs they experienced were in Ireland. Pubs tended to be a major feature of the Irish family holiday because most could rustle up a round of soups and sandwiches at a time when restaurants were few and pricy, and the only fast-food outlets in the country were the chippers. In its summer holiday special issue of early 1965, the *RTÉ Guide*'s suggestions for the ideal family holiday included boating on the Shannon, taking a cottage in Kerry, soaking up the culture of Kilkenny city, or joining the throngs of natives and Americans by the Lakes of Killarney.

While hitchhiking campers from the continent were becoming a more common sight during the summer, the native Irish were more inclined to keep a comfortable distance between themselves and the sodden ground in a hired caravan. Caravan parks boomed throughout the decade in coastal resorts like Ballybunion, Courtown, Kilkee, Tramore and Bundoran. A heavily promoted halfway house between the family-sized tent and the caravan was Air Camping. Claiming to sleep two adults and two children, the Air Camp was a tent that perched on the roof of 'any type of saloon except convertibles'. Prospective holidaymakers were informed: 'You can prepare the bed before leaving and you will find it ready for use on arrival. Allows you to rest five feet from the ground avoiding dampness, insects and dust.' The inhabitants of this wind-blown Atlantic rock weren't buying it.

The number of British and continental tourists arriving in Ireland grew hugely from the middle of the decade, as the B&I, British Rail and Normandy ferry lines competed to put on new services with bigger and better new car-transporting vessels. Between 1965 and 1968, for instance, British Rail Ferries quadrupled the number of cars and passengers travelling the Dun Laoghaire-to-Holyhead route. The traffic ran both ways, and for countless Irish children of the Sixties, their first holiday abroad was to places like Liverpool, Manchester or Coventry, often to stay with relatives who had emigrated a generation or two earlier.

As the decade wore on, a new phrase began to appear with ever-greater frequency around the dinner table and in the newspapers. It was 'traffic jam'. Each summer was pronounced the 'worst ever' as the ferries spilled out increasing volumes of tourist vehicles to swell the numbers of Irish family cars. Although the authorities had begun to clamp down on the Irish custom of abandoning parked cars wherever they liked, the habit was proving hard to break.

The ferries also brought a fresh wave of British visitors to Ireland's favourite holiday camp, Butlin's in Mosney, County Meath. During the 1960s many families returned to Butlin's year after year, drawn by the certainty of on-tap entertainment, well-policed fairground attractions, clean, unfussy chalet accommodation, a good child-minding service, and the peace of mind that you knew at the outset, more or less, how much the whole thing was going to cost.

Sir William Heygate Edmund Colborne 'Billy' Butlin had opened his Mosney camp in the late 1940s, not for the Irish, but to provide an escape for hungry English visitors from the stringent post-war rationing which would last well into the 1950s. Butlin told Ireland's media: 'I hope to charter a boat which will sail from either Fishguard or Liverpool each week taking all my holiday makers together. This camp will be entirely different from my other ventures. It is not my aim to transplant a bit of Wigan to Southern Ireland. I am going to provide a real Irish holiday for those who want it. All the staff and the bands will be Irish. Food will be a speciality. The holiday makers will be fed as it is impossible to feed them in England.'

And food was the key for British visitors who'd seen their diet allowances actually shrink since the end of the Second World War. Butlin's served up plentiful steak, pork, chicken and butter, and as many sweets, chocolates, cakes and ice creams as the war-weary British visitors could gorge on.

Billy Butlin's plans quickly came to fruition and Butlin's Mosney opened on the County Meath coast at the same time as a rival Irish-owned camp began taking guests a few miles down the coast at Red Island beside the north Dublin seaside town of Skerries.

Captain Patrick Giles, a Fine Gael TD, vented his anger through the pages of the *Catholic Standard* in an outburst headlined 'Holiday Camp And Morals'. He asserted: 'Holiday camps are an English idea and are alien and undesirable in an Irish Catholic country – outside influences are bad and dangerous.' Unable to prevent Butlin's Mosney from opening, Giles and some allies in the Catholic Hierarchy secured the concession that a church would be built right outside its main gate, with a chaplain as the moral policeman in residence.

Butlin's Mosney was an instant hit, and by the start of the 1960s was deeply woven into the social fabric of a hinterland stretching from Belfast to Dublin and beyond. It and a handful of smaller holiday camps provided regimented entertainment for the social class described by one *Irish Times* wag as 'the frayed collar worker'. Another writer in the same paper countered accusations that they were dens of vice, arguing that the chock-a-block schedule of daily activities meant that 'the first prerequisite of casual liaisons, boredom, is absent'. He concluded that the family-friendly holiday camps were citadels of family values.

At the height of its popularity in 1968, Butlin's Mosney 'right on the edge of the Irish Sea', sought bookings for 'The All-Inclusive holiday with no extras to pay'. The appeal of the camp for kids and their parents was neatly summed up in a single short paragraph that said: 'Butlin's is fabulous for the children. You can relax because they'll be enjoying themselves completely with their friends the Redcoats or taking in all the free rides in the Amusement Park that would ordinarily cost two shillings or one shilling or perhaps boating on the shallow lake or skating on the rink.'

Remarkably, the advertisement left out all mention of the single thing about Butlin's Mosney that impressed kids the most – the big underwater window onto the swimming pool was a fabulous feature associated in most young minds with the lair of a scheming Bond villain.

Girls need to be restrained

Excerpted from *Preparing A Children's Party* (1965), an edition of the *Encyclopaedia Britannica* Advisory Guides For Parents

INTRODUCTION: GIRLS NEED TO BE RESTRAINED

More than anything else the size of your accommodation limits the size of your party. Too many children crammed into a small room soon begin to bicker and squabble. In a short time only the fittest and sharpest elbows survive. Girls, with their built-in hostess-with-the-mostest ambitions, particularly need to be restrained from elaborate and impractical ideas and last-minute additions to the guest list.

THE FIRST HALF-HOUR OF A PARTY IS VITAL

Decide well in advance on the first game – a get-together cumulative one, such as Musical Bumps, Hunt The Slipper, Tig or Junior John Paul Jones, into which new hands can be introduced as they arrive. Parents delivering their offspring should be got rid of immediately and firmly (unless you want them to stay to help). Your place is with the children, not small-talking with an aimless adult who has nothing better to do than relate the story of the funny thing that happened on the way to the party. A curt instruction regarding the time to call back will get through to even the thickest-skinned.

THE LAST HALF HOUR IS ALMOST AS VITAL

A party needs rhythm and should be slowed down towards its end. No parent will thank you for handing over a truculent, screaming child who has just been extracted from some frenetic activity. It is kind to give a young child warning that he or she has been called for rather than be whisked out of a game and new interesting relationships ... If you can afford it, put waiting parents in a room and give them a drink or a cup of tea. It counts as entertainment and saves you having them for hours on end at some other time.

Ten Top TV kids' action-adventure shows

THE AVENGERS

'Always keep your bowler on in time of stress, and watch out for diabolical masterminds.' Those words of advice from Emma Peel to John Steed were pretty redundant because the spruce hero seemed immune to stress and everything the criminal masterminds could throw at him.

BATMAN

The dark knight of the original *Batman* comics was given a radical makeover in this camp and zany 1960s series which was a smash hit with Irish kids and their counterparts around the globe. Week after week arch-enemies were dispatched with a Pow! and a Zap!, while the caped crusaders dispensed advice on the importance of doing homework and drinking milk.

CAPTAIN SCARLET AND THE MYSTERONS

'The finger is on the trigger, about to unleash a force with terrible powers, beyond the comprehension of man. This force we shall know as the Mysterons. This man will be our hero, for fate will make him indestructible. His name, Captain Scarlet.' State-of-the-art puppetry and special effects made this a hit with kids and parents.

THE FUGITIVE

Framed for the murder of his wife, the ever-resourceful Doctor Richard Kimble roams the United States on the trail of a mysterious one-armed man while himself staying one step ahead of pursuing lawmen. A huge hit in Ireland, *The Fugitive* regularly featured around the top of the viewing ratings.

GET SMART

This Mel Brooks' vehicle followed the slapstick adventures of the world's most bumbling spy Maxwell Smart and his glamorous love interest, Agent 99. Smart and 99 worked for the secret US organisation CONTROL which battled the forces of KAOS for thirty minutes each week.

HAWAII FIVE-O

Set in the fiftieth state of the US, this cop show followed the sleuthing adventures of Captain Steve McGarrett and his young sidekick Danny Williams. The show was a ratings-topper in Ireland, with McGarrett's catchphrase, 'Book him, Danno', entering the lexicon. Informing a defendant in a Dublin court that he would face his comeuppance, a judge cross-wired *Five-O* and *Star Trek*, declaring: 'There will be no "Beam me up, Danno" for you.'

THE MAN FROM UNCLE

James Bond creator Ian Fleming had a hand in developing this spy series, proposing the characters of Napoleon Solo and April Dancer (featured in the spin-off *The Girl From UNCLE*). The Soviet Illya Kuryakin gave the UNCLE organisation a cooperative element during the Cold War.

MISSION: IMPOSSIBLE
The prologue for each episode featured team leader Jim Phelps taking his instructions from a tape, which would inevitably 'self-destruct in five seconds'. Phelps' team for the first series consisted of top model Cinnamon, electronics genius Barney, strongman Willy and 'man of a million faces' Rollin.

ROBIN HOOD
Robin Hood, Robin Hood, riding through the glen and shooting arrows with deadly accuracy, protects England from the scheming of Prince John and the Sheriff of Nottingham. Featuring a British cast, the show was fittingly scripted by blacklisted American writers camouflaged with false names.

THE SAINT
'Smooth-talking adventurer Simon Templar, aka The Saint, goes in where angels fear to tread. Always where the action is, he courts danger with a smile, but his charm masks a skilled fighter. The Saint always on a mission of mercy or intrigue, with a beautiful handmaiden close by.'

Architecture & Morality: the outdoor swimming pool

Families gathered at the Cabra Baths on hot summer days, but only the boys and men were allowed in the pool

Gone, but not entirely forgotten, the bracing, no-frills outdoor swimming pool was a much-loved feature of a great many 1960s Irish childhoods. There were scores of indoor public baths scattered around the country, many dating from Victorian times. Apart from the fun and games they provided, these also served the cause of public hygiene in a land where a bath in every household was far from a given, and taking a hot sudsy shower in the home was something most people only saw in films. In the Lotus Eaters segment of *Ulysses*, James Joyce has Leopold Bloom visit Dublin's Tara Street public baths for a wash and clean, and in the 1960s a visit to Tara Street for many inner-city kids doubled as both a treasured treat and the weekly bath night. The same ritual was played out all around the country every evening and weekend.

The nation's many outdoor public swimming pools served much the same function, only perhaps more so. Between coming to power in 1932, and the economic shutdown forced by the outbreak of the Second World War, the Fianna Fáil government of the mid-1930s had embarked on a programme of knocking down slums and sometimes transplanting entire communities into new housing estates. The outdoor swimming pool was seen as a good way of sitting cleanliness next to Godliness at the heart of these new communities, forming a neat dovetail of architecture and morality.

Fianna Fáil's Sean T. O'Kelly snipped the ribbon at the opening of one of these new developments in Tullamore in 1938. It consisted of 146 modern houses and a swimming pool. He told his audience: 'Our population is not increasing in the way it should and we shall have to provide houses in sufficient quantities – if housing is an encouragement, and I think it is – to encourage more and more of our young people to marry at an early age, and make the population of this country what it should be, and what it was less than a century ago.'

The swimming pool was of the windblown open-air type, freezing during the winter but merely bracing on a typical Irish summer's day. The water in the pool was treated but not heated. As one newspaper reported: 'The pond has several springboards and is equipped with the latest machinery for filtering and cleansing the water and an inflow from a river in the vicinity that changes the water every four hours.'

The new development in Tullamore offered proof positive that the Irish nation could better itself. The writer continued approvingly: 'It is most gratifying to learn from the report of the County Medical Officer of Health that the results of the slum clearance policy in Tullamore prove that when people from insanitary dwellings obtain new houses they keep them in a clean and orderly condition. The changes that have taken place in Tullamore in the conditions of living can be measured by recalling to mind the spectacle of the old, dilapidated, insanitary hovels that have been cleared away.'

However, a leading churchman felt that the poor, even given a bite of the carrot, could not be trusted to be on their best behaviour without the whack of the stick. When Reverend G. Cooney took the podium, 'he suggested that, apart from the rent collector, the Urban Council might appoint a female counterpart to supervise the domestic upkeep of the buildings and ensure that they are kept in a clean and sanitary condition. Many of the new residents who have been slum dwellers will require a little coaching or, perhaps occasionally, a knock of the stick to remind them that it is their duty to care for and preserve the amenities that have been given to them.'

By the start of the 1960s these outdoor pools had become a focus of community activity across the country, and in some places the heavy hand of clerical oversight held sway. At the Cabra Baths on the outskirts of Dublin city, for instance, while boys and girls and family groups gathered in their hundreds on hot summer days, only the boys and men were permitted to bathe in the pool. For the sake of modesty, girls were banished a short distance away to swim at the Silver Spoon, a leafy bend in the River Tolka which fed directly into the pool. Sweet vendors and ice-cream vans would add to the carnival atmosphere, together with hawkers selling plastic sandals for the benefit of the women and girls who had to cope with a riverbed covered in sharp stones.

The popularity of the Cabra Baths as a family attraction suffered in the early Sixties as gangs of what were called juvenile delinquents fought sometimes bloody turf wars for possession of the facility. By the end of the decade, in a story repeated across the country, new indoor heated pools had begun to lure parents and children away, relegating the Cabra Baths to a playground for ruffians, fly-tippers and cider parties. In the early 1980s the baths went the way of most others when they were bulldozed and filled in.

Select Bibliography and Sources

BOOKS

Children's Britannica. Advisory Guides For Parents. (*Encyclopaedia Britannica*)

Christian Brothers. *Courtesy For Boys And Girls* (M. H. Gill & Son)

Farmar, Tony. *Ordinary Lives* (A&A Farmar)

Fitzpatrick, J. *Three Brass Balls* (The Collins Press)

Horgan, John. *Irish Media: A Critical History.* (Routledge)

Leyden, Maurice. *Boys & Girls Come Out To Play.* (Appletree Press)

Lydon, John. *No Irish, No Blacks, No Dogs.* (St Martin Press)

McLoone, MacMahon (eds). *Television And Irish Society* (RTÉ-IFI)

Molloy, Martin. *The Book of Irish Courtesy* (Mercier Press)

Oram, Hugh. *The Advertising Book* (M. O. Books)

Pine, Richard. *2RN* (Four Courts Press)

Tobin, Fergal. *The Best of Decades* (Gill & Macmillan)

NEWSPAPERS AND PERIODICALS

Creation

Irish Housewife

Irish Independent

Irish Press

The Irish Times

Kilkenny People

Radio Times

RTV/RTÉ Guide

Sunday Review

OTHER SOURCES

Central Statistics Office Household Budget Inquiry for 1965–1966.

Council of Education. *The Function of the Primary School.* Government publication, 1954.

Council of Education. *The Curriculum To Be Pursued In The Primary School.* Government publication, 1954.

Department of Education. Intermediate Certificate papers.

Department of Labour. *Careers For Boys And Girls.* Government publications, 1969.

National Library of Ireland.

Historical Debates, Houses of the Oireachtas.

National Archives.